MW01242588

Many of us can relate to some degree of Job's story in the bible. He was chosen by God to be tested and went through much adversity, even ridiculed by his wife and friends about how he should curse God because of his suffering and losses. However, Job withstood the test, passed the test, and was rewarded in the latter by God. God restored Job with not only restoration (what he had), but also recompense (more than what he had previously). Many of us today have a Job-like story. I pray that this book encourages you to be BOLD in the face of adversity and trials. Know that God is perfecting your story and that you too are one of God's masterpieces for the kingdom.

"After Job had prayed for his friends, the Lord restored his fortunes and gave him twice as much as he had before." Job 42:10 NIV

Dr. Angella Banks

Disclaimer

For bulk purchases or corporate premium sales, call the office at 1.888.983.1672 or email angellabanks@xcellenceinc.org

INTRODUCTION

As we live life, we quickly discover that it is one of ups and downs, good and bad days; yet it is one that we treasure daily as a gift from God for blessing us to see another day. After Co-Authoring two books prior in 2020 and 2021, I thought my assignment was done, until God released the title, "From Broken Pieces to Masterpieces." I noted it within my phone as I often do when God gives me messages. It remained there until God gave me instructions that this was the title for my third Co-Authored book project.

I must admit with my busy schedule and active projects, I was like no way God, I just do not have the time and capacity. Unlike many, I realized that my obedience to the voice of God is what has sustained me, blessed me, and carried me in and through my life's journey of brokenness. So, in other words, I quickly got over myself as I quoted my own words back to myself, "It's not about you, build a bridge and get over yourself. You are called to lead and serve!"

As I began to read through each of these ladies' stories, I was moved to tears. "My God, what if I wasn't obedient to the call of this assignment," I said to myself silently? Each of these ladies went to the depths of their soul to release what was yet silent within. I cannot begin to imagine the amount of fear, resistance, shame that came across their minds as I am sure they pondered over and over about what to give to the world and what to keep deep within. I am beyond proud of each of them for their transparency, vulnerability, and victory to be an overcomer through life's situations with God as their anchor and guide.

Within this book, the Co-Authors share testimonies of overcoming divorce, addiction, loneliness, teen pregnancy, sickness, and lack of self-love to name a few. The anointing, strength, and power exuberated throughout this book is astonishing. Twelve ladies from all walks of life, different cities, and countries came together to inspire, uplift, encourage, and share in unity a clarion call that God specializes in broken pieces and only he can turn your life, your story, and your journey into His own masterpiece.

I pray that you enjoy this book and powerful read as you continue to embark upon life's unknown paths. Lastly, always remember, that you are a piece of art, and that you are God's masterpiece in the earth.

Dr. Angella Palmer-Banks

Table of Contents

Serenia M. Smalls-Bonds

Serenia is a native of Flint, Michigan, a United States
Marine Corps Veteran, a Certified Spiritual Life Coach,
and a Licensed Minister. She currently serves as the
National Vice-President of Sisters in Xcellence, and the
Vice President of S.L.I.C.E. (Sisters Lifting Individuals in
Confidence and Empowered).

My desire is to bring enjoyment to God and to live for his
pleasure.

Email: sereniasb@gmail.com

I AM GOD'S MASTERPIECE

Sitting on the bench of a bus stop was not an uncommon thing. It was in fact, a necessity for that particular mode of transportation. The rain was steady and cold that day and I noticed that none of the waiting passengers had umbrellas. Some protected themselves by using their jackets to cover their heads, only to leave most of their backsides exposed to the dampness. Others stood with both hands in their pockets and shoulders drawn up to their ears. I offered my seat to an elderly gentleman, but he waived his hand in refusal and pointed in the direction of the slowly approaching #42 bus.

The others noticed it too and began to form a line in anticipation of boarding. The bus emitted a strong, oily scent of exhaust fumes, hissing as its front end was lowered and the door opened. Not very many people got off at the stop which allowed the damp to huddle a quick reprieve from the elements. All but two people boarded the #42 bus and were now on their way to their various destinations. The older gentleman and I sat in silence. I thought, no wonder he didn't want my seat; he had no intention of getting on that bus.

You see, this bus stop was in front of the largest inner-city homeless shelter in St. Louis. Earlier that day, I called all over town looking for a safe place to lay my head. The first place required that I have at least one child with me. Praise God, my two boys were living with my mother at the time. The next place was for homeless married couples. I cringed at the thought of being married and homeless, but I guess there are all kinds. The other places were either already at capacity or they required their applicants to have been evicted from their homes. Then I remembered a place that had fewer restrictions and held 300. When I worked for Joyce Meyer Ministries, we provided showers and haircuts for some of their male residents. We also partnered with them in other homeless outreach and community efforts, so I was familiar with their guidelines. The only requirement was that you be in the line at 6pm when the doors opened.

So, there I sat waiting. I was hungry, cold, wet, and ashamed. The despair that engulfed me was almost unbearable. How could I have done this to myself again? I knew that I was a child of the Most High God, but there I was at rock bottom. It seemed as if I had been sitting there for hours. Just then, I noticed the man reached into his coat pocket and took out a large face watch with a frayed military styled band. Squinting intently at its face, he leaned over and asked me if I could tell him what time it was. I said, "5:45," with a sigh of relief. Almost simultaneously, the noisy, unruly, awaiting crowd began to rush towards the entrance.

I felt bad for leaving the old man at the bus stop, but hey, I had to get into this shelter! It was getting dark, and I had nowhere else to go. I jumped up, grabbed my rolling suitcase, and hurried to get in line. Luckily, I was granted entry into what the "regulars" referred to as the _Castle on the Hill._

Once inside the old Roman-styled entryway, we were given a wristband with a number on it. They instructed the men to go down to the lower level while guiding the women to an old rickety elevator in groups of 25. I saw old and young women of all ethnicities. Some were pregnant, some had several children, some were so worn and tired from the hardships of their circumstances that it showed on their faces.

I was one of them. Just 24 hours before, I was fully engaged in the madness of my addiction and sleeping outside on the sidewalk. The elevator stopped on the 5th floor, and we were escorted out by a stately looking woman with smooth skin and a thick Jamaican accent. She told us our bed was the number on our wristband. "Welcome home ladies," she said with a laugh!

The large room was split, single women on one side and women with children on the other. The workers treated us like animals. The way they distributed our hygiene items was similar to the way former President 45 threw paper towels at the residents of Puerto Rico following the devastation of Hurricane Florence.. We had to go down to the cellar with only our towels and shower shoes to an open-bay type of setting. There was no curtain, partition, or anything. We went in 4 at a time. The water was cold, and we only got 3 minutes to soap up front, back, and rinse.

We went back up 5 flights of stairs that night because that rickety old elevator stopped working. Once back to the sleeping quarters, we got into our night clothes and had snacks, which consisted of half a tuna sandwich and a box of apple juice. I wanted to curl up in a little ball and disappear, but there was a lady in the bunk across from mine who began singing, "Tragedies are commonplace, all kinds of diseases people are slipping away. Economies down, no place seems to be safe, but as for me, all I can say is thank you Lord for all you've done for me!" I couldn't help but begin to sing along with her.

That night, I slept much better than I had the previous night. At least I was indoors. I took my Bible from my bag and was led to Isaiah 42:16 (KJV), and it said 'I will bring the blind by the way they did not know; I will lead them in paths they have not known, I will make darkness light before them, and crooked places straight. These things I will do for them, and not forsake them.' The Word of the Lord brought me comfort despite the fact that I was responsible for being in this situation. I began to think back on the previous 48 hours and exactly how I got to this point.

During that time, I was in my 2nd marriage, and it was controlled by substance abuse and sheer insanity. Things had gotten so bad that I left him and checked myself into a 28- day drug rehabilitation program. It was suggested to me that if I truly wanted to recover, I would have to change my surrounding people, places, and things. That meant not returning to a situation if he was still using drugs. Although I knew this was true, I went back to him anyway. Two days after I got out, he came home with some crack. At first, I was strong. I held on for dear life. After a few hours, we began to argue about something, and before I knew it, I had the pipe up to my mouth. I was back on the merry-go-round. Things eventually got violent, and I ran out of the house and went to my neighbors and stayed until he left for work. I packed a suitcase and left. My plan was to call my mother and ask her to send me a bus ticket. A drug dealer that I knew saw me and asked me where I was going with that suitcase.

I told him I was going to call my mother and catch the bus out of town because I was leaving my husband. He told me he would let me use his phone and take me to the bus station, but he had a run to make first. I got in the car with him, and we took off. We stopped at his house, and he told me to come inside. He told me to leave the bag in the car because we would be right back out.

Depression was setting in. How could I ever overcome this guilt and shame? I was so angry with myself because I had blown 28-days clean and now I had to start all over again. How long could I stay clean this time? The condemnation I felt was so intense I could barely hold my head up. It felt like demons were all around me telling me that it was no use. I would never get off the stuff and that I would die addicted to crack cocaine. I could almost hear them laughing and pointing their fingers and taunting me.

Once inside his house, I couldn't help thinking that I had let everyone in my life down and the only one I had to turn to was this two-bit dope boy. I heard the enemy say that God was angry with me, and I had used up all my chances. I felt alone and I truly wanted to die. I just wanted to call my mother to come to my rescue. He showed me to a seat in the entryway and extended his phone to me. As I reached for it, he playfully withdrew it and smiled in a devilish manner. "I have a little something for you," he said. Before I could respond, he handed me a little purple velvet bag trimmed in gold. Inside was a lighter and a crack pipe already loaded. I should have just dropped it on the floor, but I didn't.

Once I took that first hit, I was off to the races. I smoked what he gave me, and I could not stop. There was no way I could call my mother or anyone else for that matter. Take it from me, the only way to control drug use is to never take the first hit. One is too many and a thousand is never enough. After a few hours of being stuck like Chuck, he finally refused to give me more crack and insisted that we leave. He wouldn't let me use his phone and he didn't take me to the bus station. Instead, he dropped me off 3 blocks from the Amtrak Train station and would not even give me $5 for something to eat. So, there I was, even further from home, tweaking and stinking. I had a hard choice to make. Do I call my mother and try to explain my plight, or do I just tuck my tail and return to my dysfunctional marriage.

I was nowhere near the bus station, so I made the 3-block walk to the train station. Because I was so high, I decided not to call my mother, but to try to get into a shelter the next day. Besides, the station was clean, well-lit, and tucked away under the I-44 overpass. I settled in on two of the bench-like seats and made myself as comfortable as I could under the circumstances. Just as I was about to nod off, the ticket agent came over the loudspeaker and said, "Attention all passengers, attention all passengers, the station will be closing after the departure of the 1:45am Texas Eagle with service to Little Rock, Dallas, Fort Worth, Austin, San Antonio..." He named a few other cities, but I was deafened by the phrase *'will be closing after the 1:45 departure.'* Closing? Where was I supposed to go? I jumped up and sprinted to the desk and asked him did he say closing? "Yes," he replied, "Do you have a ticket?" I lied and said, "Yes, but my train doesn't leave until 9am. Where am I supposed to go until then?" He looked at me and said, "I'm sorry ma'am." As he called for final boarding, I got my rolling suitcase and walked out of the door. It was 1:45 in the morning, and there I was, outside the Amtrak Station tired, hungry, and afraid. I rolled my bag out to the sidewalk under the streetlight and went to sleep.

There I was, 2 days later, safe in a shelter, showered, fed, and faced with a serious decision. Should I return to the dysfunction or make a call to my mother to rescue me from myself? I only had the Word of the Lord that said, "He would never leave me nor forsake me." I suddenly felt the peace of God and went to sleep. Three days later, the city came in and closed the shelter because the building was unsafe, causing over 200 people to be displaced. I was one of them.

As the people piled out of the facility, I overheard someone say something about the Vet Center. I looked in the direction of the voice and it was the elderly gentleman from the bus stop. He said that he was about to walk around the corner and talk to someone. I quickly caught up with him and told him that I too was a Veteran. He looked at me and smiled and said, "I knew that." I said, "How did you know?" He told me the Lord had led him to me because I was searching for something.

Immediately the tears began to well up in my eyes and I was reminded of the scripture that I had read the night before. God told me that he was going to lead me in paths not known to me! I swallowed hard and tried to ask him what his name was, but nothing would come out. The same way he waved his hand at the bus stop when I tried to offer him my seat, he did it again and said, "please stop talking and just walk." We got to the end of the block and rounded the corner; I looked up and there in big red letters was a sign that read "THE VET CENTER." For the first time in quite a while, I felt a tinge of hope. I was excited at the notion of having a place just for Veterans. It was the one time that I was truly glad that I had served in the military.

Fortunately, there were counselors available to assist me with everything from shelter to drug rehab, and to marriage counseling if I wanted it. They gave me a place to shower, and a voucher for two new outfits. They even offered to purchase my bus ticket to Tennessee if that was what I wanted. There was good hot food, a big screen TV and laundry facilities. My God had indeed come through! After in-processing, I went to look for the elderly gentleman and could not find him anywhere. Could he have been an angel?

All of this took place during a time when I was overtaken by guilt, shame, and condemnation. No matter how I tried, I just could not get over what I had done to my children, my family and to my God. It was all a result of my disobedience to His word to me concerning a thing.

About 4 years prior to all of this, I sought the Lord, and He answered me with a resounding "No!" I decided to go against His Word and His will. I did my own thing and I lost everything I had, including my 2 sons. Little did I know at the time, that I would go on to pay a very dear price for that one act of disobedience. This is just a snippet of the brokenness that I suffered. It literally took me over 12 years to get completely free from drugs and alcohol. During which time I overdosed twice, attempted suicide by stepping in front of a semi-truck on a very busy on-ramp to I-40. I was brutally beaten and nearly killed over $65 in food stamps. I was arrested for Grand theft auto, but the charges were dropped, and I was released. I even stole money from my church. I am not proud of these things and neither have I forgotten. I was guilty and in sin. I hurt a lot of people in my addiction.

But today, I am 11 years crack-free. My relationships have been mended and I have been justified by faith; therefore, I have peace with God. I once described my brokenness like a thin potato chip that had fallen to the floor, and someone stepped on it. Not a Pringles, not a Ruffles, but a Lay's. I can truly say that God turned my broken pieces to a Masterpiece.

Monica Quintero-DeVlaeminck aka
"Monica La Colombiana"

Health & Motivational Coach, Motivational Speaker, MC,
Author, and Teacher

"Behold, I am sending you out as sheep in the midst of
wolves, so be wise as serpents and innocent as doves."
Matthew 10:16 KJV

Her purpose and mission statement: Leaving gentle
footprints on people's hearts

Monica is accepting new health and motivational coaching
clients, building a team of coaches, and is taking on
motivational speaking engagements. She can be reached via

email: monica@lacolombiana.me, IG: monicaqd44,
Website: https://bit.ly/monicaqd

FB: https://www.facebook.com/groups/198018542379417/
"MLC Breaking the Chains"

I AM GOD'S MASTERPIECE

How many of us can pinpoint the exact day and time your LIFE shattered into a million pieces? For me, it was the day my beautiful mom, only 44 years old, took her final breath. I knelt by her bedside watching closely, as I held my breath waiting to see her chest rise from her next breath. I held her hand, praying for a miracle and in disbelief that CANCER was taking my mom. This beautiful, full of energy, God-fearing, infectious smile of a woman that worked so hard her whole life to give her two kids everything she could, sacrificing herself, was being taken by these little cells that were quickly multiplying throughout her tiny and fragile body.

My mom, Maria Cristina, named after her mom, was the eldest of 5, and by the time of my mom's passing, she only had two sisters left behind. I smile when I think of her, with her quirkiness and innocence. When she was nineteen, she still believed that the stork brought the babies to their new families. Her first kiss by a boy was on her cheek on her 21st birthday; she ended up getting scolded by her mom for allowing that boy to kiss her. She believed that if you had determination in your heart, you could achieve anything. My sweet mom graduated from a university called, 'Colegio Mayor de Cundinamarca' in Colombia, with an Architectural Draftsman Degree.

Even with that degree, she wasn't hired, because women did not get those types of jobs in the United States of America back in the 70's. She continued on with the determination to be successful and landed a position working for the Army, as a civil engineer.

When she was diagnosed with cancer and the doctors told her she had only six months to live, she refused to believe that, and made a point to LIVE until I was at least eighteen years old. She surpassed what the doctors said by years! My mom barely ever complained about her pain, and somehow always had a smile on her face. She was the BEST mom ever!

When your life shatters into a million pieces you either 1) jump without thinking and try to sweep up every piece, using the dustpan to collect your shattered self, just to gather it into a paper bag, or you 2) stand there in shock, stunned, hoping to wake up from the nightmare that just flashed in front of your eyes, somehow muttering in a silent whisper, to please do over and over again.

For me it was a Sunday, June 18, 1989. A moderate day, clear skies in the 60's. Everyone else was going about their business, yet I was unable to think clearly, stunned, and was wondering HOW and WHY did this happen? How was the LIFE of my mother slipping away and I was unable to do anything about it?

I graduated from high school in June 1988, and soon after graduation, my mom had encouraged me to go to school in Bogotá, Colombia. Little did I know she had more reasons for me to go there beyond school. She didn't want me to find out how truly sick she was, nor did she want me to get closer to the new boy I had fallen head over heels for. Her goal was to try to give me as normal of a childhood transition into adulthood as she could, by convincing me that improving my Spanish and other languages would be a great advantage in the world. The truth was that her cancer was getting stronger, and her body couldn't tolerate the Chemotherapy nor more surgeries.

My aunt Leonora and uncle Eduardo would come early in the mornings, they would make us kids' breakfast and lunch before we would wake up for school, allowing my mom to pretend that she was the one that did it on her own as if everything was fine. As soon as we were off to school, they would come back, clean the house, do laundry, and take her to doctor appointments. It was years after the passing of my mom, did I find out this truth. My aunt and uncle consoled me, that it was her wish to try to keep our childhood as pure as possible without the worry of her illness. I felt robbed from being able to make the choice to be by her side.

What I would've traded to have had the chance to be with her that last year of her life, knowing what I know now! I felt guilty not being there for both my mom and my brother. I found out that during the year I was gone to Colombia, my mother's illness took yet another turn for the worse and she was having seizures. My heart broke for my little brother, having to see my mom slowly deteriorate in front of him. I can only imagine how scary this was for him, being only 10 years old. Somehow, my mom found the strength and will power to overcome her new obstacles.

She still managed to get my brother involved in little league and play dates with friends.

During my year in Bogotá, Colombia, I remember in late April 1989, my uncle Manuel and aunt Barbarita, were planning their bi-annual trip to Los Llanos Orientales de Colombia. It was a sixteen-hour road trip, with some parts of the journey not so safe, and possibilities of encountering "La Guerrilla (FARC)," a revolutionary armed force. Even in knowing that, it was my favorite place to go and ride in the back of a big truck along with goats and chickens. Yet, I had this gut-wrenching feeling in the pit of my stomach that I needed to go home. Therefore, I talked with my uncle and aunt, made the plans, and called my mom to tell her I was coming home to be with her for Mother's Day. She convinced me to wait until the 4th of July and to meet in Miami with her sister and mother (another aunt and my abuelita).

My journey continued and off we went to Los Llanos to my uncle's 780 acres farm called "Rancho La Campiña." It was filled with cattle, wild anteaters, goats, howling monkeys and this cool river that streamed through the farm. Yet this feeling, this yearning about my mom kept bugging me. So much so, that after two weeks of being there, I went and spoke to my uncle about it, apologizing, but willing to take a bus back. He understood and asked if I could just wait another week or two, he would then bring me back personally. I agreed. When we finally came back, I called with the determination in my mind, ready to not, I would not allow my mom to convince me otherwise, but then her sister answered the phone. Confused, I asked if I called the wrong number, and all she said was, "Oh honey, I'm glad you called, you need to come home now."

At the Los Angeles Airport, during my final flight connection, I called home collect (back in those days we didn't have cell phones, there were only pay phones connected to walls, where you put money into it or call collect, where the other person receiving would pay up to 3 times more just to connect, not to mention the long-distance costs). I was 18 and new at traveling and venturing alone in the vast world, especially in coming back to the United States of America from Colombia, South America.

As I think back to this day, I'm riddled with guilt because I allowed my young flirty inclination to use the excuse that the call was too costly, thinking we would have plenty of time to talk when I finally arrived home. I said, "Mom, don't worry, I'll be home soon, and we'll be able to talk. I love you…. Bye." My mom tried to convince me that she didn't care about the cost, but I insisted, as I hung up and walked towards the cute guy that walked past me and smiled. Even as I sat writing these words, my eyes welled up with tears as I reflected upon how inconsiderate and immature I was back then.

When I finally arrived home, after being gone for almost a year, it was no longer the home that I knew when I left. It looked like a hospital setting where the living room once stood, and my room was all packed into boxes and stuffed into a closet. I could feel the stuffiness of the house as it was filled with people and chaos. I saw my mom laying helpless in a hospital bed, drugged with morphine and unable to communicate. That's when life slapped me in the face with reality. My heart sank and my once strong vibrant mother that could fight and withstand anything the doctors said, was coming to an end. Did I give into the world's reality? Did I forget my belief in God? Did I give up on miracles?

Today, those next three days are still a blur to me, but there was one moment that filled my heart and gave me hope. That hope was in WHO Jesus is, and the fact that He still lives. After a while there was quietness, and I was finally alone with my mom, when suddenly my mom's eyes stared straight up towards the ceiling, and she began to smile. I still remember that smile. It warms my heart to think of that moment. It was one of those smiles that made her forget all her pain, sorrows, and worries. I asked with a sense of comfort, "Mom, what do you see?" She replied, "Puppies, oooh, it's so beautiful here… I see Jesus." As soon as she said, "Jesus," the room was filled with a strong scent of roses. I looked all around, windows were closed, no doors opened, no flowers in the house at all. I received this overwhelming feeling that everything would be okay. Yet I still wondered how my precious mom was being taken away.

The night the coroners took my mom's body away, the evening sky was so clear. I stood outside and watched the coroner's vehicle disappear in the distance. I was numb, my brain was trying to understand what had just happened.

In the distance of the majestic blue sky, a streak of white went through the horizon, right from where the coroner's car disappeared. It ascended upward in an angle, as if it was going towards heaven. My aunt Pilar grabbed my arm and said, "There goes your mom, straight to heaven." I didn't want my mom to leave. I needed her here. How was I going to do "LIFE" without her? How was I going to follow through with everything she had spoken to me about in past years?

I made many mistakes, and it took me several falls with my face in the gravel until finally, I started putting into practice what my precious mom spent all her time trying to prepare me for. As I slowly started to sweep up my broken pieces, I realized I wasn't alone. Each time I fell, and each time I turned to face the world and took a step towards it, this presence kept luring me back to God. I had promised my mom two things, 1) to stay connected to my brother and 2) to not stop going to church. Many times, I felt as if I failed her, as if she was looking down at me from heaven with disappointment. You see, I believe my mom can see me from heaven due to a story in the Bible, Luke 16:19-30. The story of a rich man and a poor man that both died, one sent to Hades, and the other comforted by Father Abraham and they could see each other from either place. I also believe that my mom is like an angel, due to Matthew 22:30, "For in the resurrection they neither marry nor are given in marriage but are *like angels* in heaven."

If my story resonates with you at all, I'm here to tell you that you are not alone. God is right there by your side. I will tell you that you were lovingly made on purpose, and for a purpose. That we might live in the world, but that we are not of the world. We belong to God, and He tells us in Proverbs 3:5-6 "...do not lean on your own understanding. In all your ways acknowledge Him, and He will make straight your paths." I finally started realizing that He's been waiting for me this whole time with open arms. GOD will put your broken pieces back together again if you let Him. Like in Luke 15:7-32, where the prodigal son returns, God our Father patiently and lovingly awaits for our return to Him, because He loves us so.

As I slowly gather my broken pieces with Jesus by my side. God is slowly creating a Masterpiece within me. You see, art is a constant job of creative imagination, filled with beauty from the scars of life and emotions, which takes time. As time progresses, the masterpiece changes, incorporating every aspect of your life. Through joy with each laugh, the crinkle of your nose and wrinkles around your eyes, even your sorrows as each tear flowed, leaving a mark that was felt and seen by God himself. Not everyone knows how to appreciate art, much less a masterpiece like yourself. Don't sell yourself short, you get more valuable as time goes on. Remember, Jesus paid for you with His LIFE, because to Him, you are priceless. Let's go out and be the Magnum Opus that God created us to be. Are you ready?

What chains in life have been keeping you prisoner from your full potential? What is the purpose that God has given you? Is there a dream waiting to escape and become a

reality? Are you *REALLY* ready? Start with a baby step and join my FB group: MLC Breaking the Chains
https://www.facebook.com/groups/198018542379417/

Monica Dunnagan PhD, E. Ds,
Counselor, Psychology Professor

Author, Speaker, Consultant and Author

Monica holds a PhD in Psychology from Walden
University in Public Administration & Social Change

Christ said, "he will never leave us". I believe this with all
my being. The key to healing is believing in our Lord and
Savior and that he will never leave us. I believe and always
will believe that Christ is my protector, even when I feel
broken. No matter how much or how little you have; I have
learned that God gives you what you need, while he works
in you! Thank you, God!

www.dunnaganconsultantsgroup.com

I AM GOD'S MASTERPIECE

God has laid a message on my heart that I will share with you throughout my chapter, thus moving us further beyond the "Broken Pieces." There is a greater reason why so many women from across the globe have been chosen to share their stories through this "Masterpiece." The reason is to touch the lives of others through hope, caring, the sharing of Gods words and prayers. It is my hope that each of you reading these passages look deep into your heart and feel the love of Christ through everyone's chosen words.

Not once have I ever asked God why I endured such pain and suffering, to include any new suffering, because I knew there was a reason. I continue to be faithful and ask God, "What's next?" You see just like Job; God knows how best to use his children to teach others. It does not matter how rich, poor, humble, or desolate you are, God will show you what is next if you listen. The Lord knows who we are, what we think, and what we are going through every minute of the day, even when Satan is at the forefront.

A perfect example lies in the passages of Job 1:12 "the lord said unto Satan, behold all that he hath is in thy power; only upon himself put not forth thine hand..." KJV. Satan did as God commanded, and Job lost everything he had, except for his love of Christ. Job never once lost his faith, nor did he ask God why. Later God would allow Satan to stricken Job with boils all over his body, but Job never once asked God why. Neither should we ask why. Instead, we should seek God's guidance in the lessons he is teaching us.

I grew up in a small community, small church, and in an area where you could run, play, and visit friends without worry of being intentionally hurt. Not like today where crime rates are rising even in our young children, no matter where you live. I left that small community too young and too naïve and landed right in the middle of a cycle of abuse that left me broken. A rollercoaster ride to hades that could only end when I decided to jump.

However, it is not always as easy as simply jumping ship, sometimes you need a stronger force than you are to help you take that leap. Your torcher will isolate you from your family and from any type of life that includes outside assistance. People will see signs and not assist, due to fear of not knowing how. Your torcher will find you no matter where you run to. Therefore, life as you know it seems helpless and hopeless. No one responds to the signals you are sending off due to fear of not knowing the consequences. Yes, I have seen it all. Seen people turn away from me and not assist me until I was broken into silence.

It took me way too long to understand that God could help me when others could not. After a great deal of contemplation, I knew that God was the only way out, that no one else would come to my rescue. I truly believed that God had greater plans for me and that he would hold my hand while I jumped and began a new journey. I believed that He would protect my children. I am thankful every day that God pulled me away and guided me on to a greater life. Notice that I referred to "God guiding" me, you, or us, because it is still up to you to do your part in that journey. You must seek God's guidance to fully grasp his strength. You are not a victim; you are a child of God! You are a survivor, a creator of life, and an agent of change in others!

It was not easy once I made that decision. I was stalked, harassed, and even tormented for months after I left, until one day a new lawyer right out of school said, "Let me help," and he did. I was terrified; my lawyer showed up in a wrinkled shirt, but he represented me, and the judge agreed that I should be safe and ordered my ex to stay away from me. At that point, he finally left me alone. That day I learned to never judge a book by its cover, because that man in that wrinkled shirt saved my life.

This did not mean I was free from other evil ways, it just meant I was stronger and more aware of the evil of others. Being broken can occur many times in a person's life span and often more than once. As you notice, I will repeat this statement many times. Why? Because life is not perfect, and every day is not guaranteed; so live life everyday as you are a child of God.

Just as I pulled all of what I had left in me to survive; Job stood by his faith and trusted God and in Job 42:10 KJV, "The Lord gave Job twice as much as he had before." Today I live an easier life. I work when I want, and I can take leisure time as well, all because of God's greater plan for me. The most valuable aspect I have is that I ask God, "What is next?" "Where do you want me to work?" And lastly, "What shall I do for your glory?

Always stand alert because Satan, the greatest of all fallen angels, still listens to God. He may roam the earth to and fro, but he also seeks God's counsel, even though God sent him away. The thought of Satan may make you take a moment to think about why God would allow Satan to taunt Job. Just like God allowed me to stay in a bad situation. Why? To make me stronger, but most of all to show me how to grow a strong relationship with him. I find it important to always believe, be humble and grateful, but most of all know that God will guide you through any storm that stands in your path. Know that a life of "Broken Pieces" can occur at any point and time in one's life (see, are you getting the point?). Just like Job, it can be a whirlwind of destruction and grief, but also a whirlwind of uplifting and praise.

> *Think about what your most "broken" journey was and then ask; was God testing me? Will this be the only "broken" time in my life?*

Acknowledging that you have "Broken pieces" can allow a person to begin a slow journey to masterpieces, through prayer and by recognizing signals that help is needed. I state slow, because healing without God is not an easy process. Learning with God is diving deep into God's word to find your own level of peace. Whether it is your own despair or someone else's, life takes new forms when prayer and God's wisdom are sought out.

Throughout my life's journey I have met the faces of solitude and emptiness, but I have also been filled with wisdom and knowledge. Growth both mentally and spiritually out of the darkness that once surrounded me. Through this, I have realized that while it is vital to continue the right path; I must reach out to others who are struggling as well. God is always ready to shine His light on us and through us to help others see His glory.

I want to point out that struggling with feelings of hopelessness and despair are distress signals for help. Have you ever watched a drug addict reach for another hit, then push it away? That is a sign for help. Have you read a note by a loved one who wants nothing more than to die? Again, these are signals for help. Prayer and seeking God's wisdom can change lives forever and pull someone out of their dark place.

Working in prison reform, I meet these challenges daily. We see more and more younger aged individuals entering the prison system, for gang related activities, drugs, theft, and more. What has happened to our environments, our communities? These kids need our support and God's teachings, yet they only receive emptiness at home and neglect at school. Don't get me wrong, I am overjoyed that God placed me where I am, so I can help others turn their lives around. Sometimes a person only needs to know that their life matters and it matters enough to earn even the smallest amount of respect. However, one can only wonder why; why are they truly there?

We do not judge or ask questions; we simply assist in recovery, learning and moving forward to a more successful productive life upon release. There is no greater feeling than helping someone reset their thinking pattern. Just by resetting their belief system, I am blessed to watch their change take place before my eyes. Thus, making any pain gone through previously little to nothing. That is what God's glory does to me and for others!

I want to make a reference to a book that I recently read: "When Women Pray." I do so to state this; I believe that when women pray the world changes! When women come together and pray for the greater good or a greater life; God listens, and God gives his help and gives over to their needs. This does not mean that men do not pray just as strong, but when I read this book, it simply brought reality to my eyes. T.D. Jakes "When Women Pray", reviews women from the bible who through prayer changed their fate and led others to believe that their own "Broken Pieces" can turn into "Masterpieces" when they seek God's counsel through prayer. This book has helped me through the accepting process of my husband's cancer journey: my new brokenness to masterpiece!

If you recall, I stated earlier that "brokenness" can occur many times through our life span. Two years ago, I noticed changes in my husband's behavior and his cognitive processes but was not sure what was wrong. He would not talk about anything that concerned him. Why should he? He was the man that could take care of anything and by admitting to something was wrong would mean that he was weak (in his eyes at least). My husband is anything but weak. He is strong, healthy, loving, and compassionate; a man who wants to care for his family in every way possible. However, his health was getting in the way of that process.

God allows us to feel pain, suffering, and the feeling of being alone. Why? So, we will grow closer to him! I learn more and more every day, that when trouble arises, to turn to his word. I always have a bible close to me because I have learned that when something is wrong and I feel all the crazy sensors going off, I need to read Gods words for comfort and for guidance, no matter where I am. God teaches us to pray continuously throughout our day, because this will assist us on our journey back to him.

I read the most wonderful piece the other day where the author was speaking on our life after death. He mentioned that we are seeking the wrong path, because life beyond the clouds was not our destination, but the new earth was. While I read this information, I could see the new earth almost as if it was within my reach. Green trees, grass, wildflowers, and animals roaming free. Most like where I reside currently. A place that is untouched and animals are protected. Can you imagine such a place, where crime does not exist and everything, every being coexists in harmony? I can! That is the future we should be working toward and looking forward to!

Well, I am at the end of my chapter, but I could go on for days about the gifts of God! I want to leave you with this thought. In Jeremiah 1:5 KJV, "Before I formed thee in the belly, I knew thee; and before thou comest forth out of the womb I sanctified thee, and I ordained thee a prophet unto nations." We were sanctified in utero, however, once we were born, we were born unto a world of sin! A world of hate! A world of crime! Our job today is to lead others back to Christ! Back to a world of sanctuary!

I want to give my photographer a note of thanks for taking the time to capture me! She is a child of God!

Thank you, Natalie Affourtit Photography: natalieaffourtit@gmail.com , for assisting me in finding the right photo for this book. A new and rising entrepreneur!

Dr G.W. Dyson Nierszhauss

(Known by her friends as simply 'Alannah')

Academic, Author, Medical Researcher, Health Educator and Corporate Consultant, currently involved with Human Performance, Longevity, and Spiritual Healing.

Dr Dyson is the President and Co-Founder of 'Dyson Therapeutics' offering Integrative Medicine, Optimizing Cognitive, Emotional, Physical and Spiritual Performance, Pain Management, Weight Loss, Anti-aging, Recovery & Restorative Therapies.

Dyson Therapeutics: https://**hack-your-performance**.dysontherapeutics.com

https://linktr.ee/DrGWDyson

Phone (647) 885 4809

Email: DrDyson@dysontherapeutics.com

I AM GOD'S MASTERPIECE

My friends, John, and Rob, joined me on New Year's Eve to discuss our upcoming trip to the enchanting Vilcabamba: the 'Valley of Longevity.' It is not uncommon for locals to reach 100 years of age. Some claim up to 120, even up to 130.

I had just returned from Shi Lanka, where I was researching the prehistoric Dambulla caves and Adam's Peak. Christians in Sri Lanka ascribe it to the place where Adam, the first Ancestor, first set foot as he was exiled from the Garden of Eden. These legends of Adam are connected to the idea that Sri Lanka was the original Eden. I had just become the CEO of a newly merged corporation, finished my second doctorate, and I was working on a journal article on epidemiology. That night, as we brought our glasses up for a toast, I thought to myself, I have achieved all the goals I set for myself. Later on, I went to bed and hugged Michie, my orange tabby cat, while she purred happily and pushed against me to gain access under the covers. I was happy.

Six days later, my friend Helene drove from Montreal without a break and called an ambulance after seeing my state on her arrival. I had a fever, difficulty breathing, and my lips were blue. At the hospital, I was soon advised to put my affairs in order. A lawyer dictated on the phone a living will, which Peter scribbled on a serviette. It was signed, witnessed, and indicated that I was not to be resuscitated or intubated. This was followed by a phone call to my siblings in Argentina, to let them know that I was in grave condition and might not recover.

We said our goodbyes and I spent a few minutes with my brother who is a pastor praying for my health and my soul. The next hour the President of the Board and two Directors visited from our corporation. They needed access to my computer codes and passwords. I believe I spent the next couple of hours grappling with the endless list of 'urgent matters to deal with', as who will take care of my pets, pay my bills, mortgage, hydro, gas, etc., at least until my demise or return home. Soon I succumbed to pneumonia and sepsis, and lost coherence and any rational thoughts. Days moved fast; day and night, night and day became one. I was on pause. Months flew off the calendar, and I remained still. I stopped fretting. I found peace, or perhaps simply the ease and effortlessness created by the slowing of the thought process.

While scrambling to hold on to those few remaining tidbits of my life still under my control there were others who had access to my room, and my body, at all times. I am still haunted by the futile attempts of nurses wrestling with needles trying to find weakened veins, and doctors draining fluid from my lungs. The procedures were agonizing, invasive and seemingly endless. But I became impervious to the pain once I resolved that no matter what I would get through this. Before long I surrendered to the experience of withdrawing from the manic world of unattended demands and responsibilities. I have struggled all my life with anxiety and restlessness, and here I was facing the most critical moment in my life. I reached peace in the midst of chaos. It was happening to my body, but it was not touching my soul.

I reminded myself that if I were condemned to die by a firing squad, whether I crawled and shivered with fear, or stood poised and collected, death was imminent, and I was better off facing my fate stoically. Once I accepted my place in this drama, I became peaceful. Pain, vulnerability, helplessness, and lack of control became the new norm. By surrendering to the process, I found a deep serenity that became my companion throughout the ordeal.

Days came and went. I started seeing beauty in little things. There was a large window, and the sun would shine on my bed for about 3 hrs. I would sunbathe my legs and arms. I was losing weight rapidly. My calves were wrinkled and parched; the skin dried up. I saw my naked body in the mirror while a PSW washed me, and I marvelled at the look of my buttocks. I thought 'they are a size of an eight-year-old child.' When I glanced at my face in the mirror, I did not recognize it. Who is this? This is not me.

As weeks went on, my awareness of body and soul as two different entities became clear. I was taken aback by this realization. I was not my body. I had considered myself as my body, but harshly criticized its imperfection. My legs were not shapely enough, my skin not taut enough, my breasts not large enough…it seemed that I was left wanting in many departments. Suddenly I was overwhelmed with emotion in the realization that this same body I had contemptuously censured had unselfishly served me for a lifetime. A feeling of regret passed through me. I felt remorse for the unquestionable cruelty of my judgement. I became aware of the beauty and the blessings it brought me: high intelligence, athleticism, strength, vitality, stamina, clear energy, and a high capacity for sustained work. I, in my humility, found myself in deep dialogue with my own body:

"Thank you, thank you. You have been there for me all along. I have only gratitude and appreciation for all you helped me accomplish and for all you made possible for me: education, travelling, sports, laughter, making love, giving birth, pleasure, pain, and healing. You stuck through it despite the little acknowledgement I ever gave you. Sorry for my thoughtlessness, and short-sightedness. Thank you for bringing love, pleasure, and joy to my world." I was overcome by still a further realization, 'that not only had my body been perfect all along, but that I would not choose another body if I had a chance to do so.' And just like that, I had, for the first time, loved my body through and through.

As it became clear that I was getting closer to meeting my creator, a friend of mine suggested if I truly wanted to live, to 'ask God to let me live.' I could not bring myself to say those words. I had already relinquished my attachment to this world. As my health deteriorated and the blood oxygen levels kept plummeting, I started asking for the hospital Chaplain. I wanted to make my peace with God and to receive the last rites. I specifically asked for a Christian Pastor or Priest, though I indicated that any denomination would do. It was after my third failed attempt at obtaining last rites that I joked with my doctor "even at my death's door I am yet to be taken seriously." The prospect of formally making peace with my creator was abandoned altogether. I found comfort in the discovery of the closeness I already held for my creator. Peace returned to my soul.

One morning, the pulmonologist (lung specialist) showed up just after 7 AM, and he told me that for the first time since I was hospitalized the inflammation in my lungs had started to subside. The oxygen level was improving. He added, 'whatever it is that you are doing, keep doing it, and keep yourself healthy. We have no idea what caused this turning point.' I received the news with consternation, for I had made peace with leaving this world, but I had yet to consider the prospect of living with a disability. My poor body was exhausted and in disrepair. It seemed like the fates decided to keep me here.

Three weeks later, early in the morning, a nurse announced that I was going to be discharged. By 11:30 AM, my suitcase was on the bed. They gave me a second tank of oxygen to take home, and a wheelchair was whisked to the bedroom to carry me to the car.

As I left the room, I started crying. The entire nightmare hit me. I was weak and dishevelled. My hair has not been washed in over a month. I was heading home in a wheelchair and on oxygen and there was no one available to help me. I was thankful yet terrified to leave the hospital. What if I run out of oxygen? How would I be able to care for myself? Would I be able to bathe myself? How was I going to manage?

Being at home again felt wonderful. I cherished my bed and delighted in the company of my cats. There were good times and hard ones. I passed out several times. I miscalculated the oxygen levels in tanks. Sometimes I was not able to prepare my meals. I became stronger. Neighbours and friends showed up and helped me bathe or with other household tasks. A month after leaving the hospital I started rehab and was strong enough to take a few steps. I was relentless. Soon, the wheelchair would become a memory. Eight months later I no longer required oxygen.

On a more sombre note, I spent the next few months wrapping up business affairs and orchestrating my withdrawal from the corporate world. I said goodbye to my former lifestyle, and the many hobbies and activities I once enjoyed. Close friends and colleagues who had been a major part of my life started to all drift away. Our worlds no longer held much in common.

Together with these losses - my sense of identity and purpose faded. I no longer knew who I was, what was I here for. Most importantly I had lost all direction for my life. Plans I have made for my future were rendered obsolete by a body that was now unable to keep up with the demands and the ominous *'you have up to 3 years to live.'* I questioned God: 'Why would you leave me on earth without a hope to recover? Why did you not let me go?' I considered suicide a way out of this misery.

One early afternoon, feeling empty inside, on my way out of the house, I caught a glimpse of myself in the mirror. I hardly recognized the person looking back at me. Lost and confused I strayed to a nearby park. The life I knew gradually grew faint and disappeared. I struggled to hold on to the memory of those I loved which was also fading. Time stopped. I was standing at the end of a world I could no longer go back to and a new world I could not see myself living in. My soul had folded in on itself and laid inert at my feet. My body, still alive, waited impatiently for a death that could not come fast enough.

Later that day, I was following a smoky trail into the woods and beheld a soldier sitting by a fire inside a circular spiral of intertwined tree limbs and branches. It was the size of a large room, and the limbs were as thick as a person's leg. Upon noticing me, he bid me come and sit by the fire. As we became acquainted, he told me of how a difficult divorce and the loss of contact with his daughter led him to self-destruction, drugs, and alcohol. Building this circular spiral became his healing journey back to the creator. He found once more his love of God. I began to cry, and he offered me a spot to recline. Weak and exhausted, I leaned back. Consumed in darkness I fell asleep.

I dreamed that *"in an outburst of anger, I ran through the woods. I wanted to tear my heart out and throw it away. Shedding final tears for that sterile heart while preparing to leave it behind, I see the rocks, plants and weeds dancing and singing, full of delight and joy. Such was the boundless love remaining in my heart that bliss had flooded them. Suddenly, I wavered in my intent to walk away.*

Beauty overwhelms in its rapture, the sacred presence of God returning to my soul, the spirit renewed and reborn with unparalleled love touching the very core of my being and flooding the recesses of my mind, transmuting pain into blessings, and making life one with God's love." I woke up to the crackling noise of the smouldering fire.

Shades of green, brown and sky in my surroundings created a paradise of unrivalled beauty. With renewed life and vitality, I walked to the nearby creek. The wealth of salmon moving upside current side by side to spawn and create new life as they are soon to leave this world. Sunlight breaks into a rainbow of glittering colours on the creek's surface. I smile. Beauty and Joy flood my heart as it bursts to open into an abundance of unconditional love. My creator is present. Love and Life are accessible to me again. God's Grace blesses me once more.

Epilogue: I reclaimed the will to live in finding beauty. I opened Dyson Therapeutics (Longevity Medicine). I walk 23 Km twice a week. I am in remission and disability-free.

Mrs. Christy Dawn Harris

Founder and Owner of Healthy Bizness, Holistic
Entrepreneur Fitness Motivator

My Heart + My Passion + My Ministry

"Healthy Life Happy Life"

I can do all things through Christ who gives me strength

Philippians 4:13 KJV

Christy Dawn Harris is a Holistic Entrepreneur and
Certified Coach with Xcellence Leadership Coaching Firm.
She uses her passion to empower others to reach their
greatness and unlimited potential. She is also the owner of
Healthy Bizness. Healthy Bizness is an entrepreneurial
platform that speaks to the whole person in health,
wellness, and beauty.

healthybiznesscoach@gmail.com

I AM GOD'S MASTERPIECE

Life on this earth is something that is precious, and the time given is valuable. Each day is a day to be thankful because you are created for a reason and God makes no mistakes. The plan that God has for you is your individual journey, therefore trust that all will be well in all situations.

The Lord is my strength and my shield, my heart trust in Him, and He helps me. My heart leaps for joy, and with my song I praise Him. Psalm 28:7 KJV

You will encounter many tests for your testimony and what I like to call opportunities along the way that can create change within and out. Remember You are God's beautiful, created masterpiece. Each day that you are blessed with, is a day to be cherished and to be thankful for.

God is the same yesterday, and today and forever. Hebrews 13:8 KJV

When I've faced challenging moments in my life that scripture has been a reminder to me that God still heals. He is a miracle worker, He is faithful, and He can still do a suddenly in my life.

In April 2020, days after the birth of my daughter I became extremely sick with pneumonia and had extreme trouble breathing. After several breathing treatments and increased oxygen, my breathing was getting worse and not better. At that time, I was in one hospital room, and my daughter was in another hospital room across the hall from me, being cared for by a nurse.

My husband could not be at the hospital with us, because I was no longer there for the birth of our child. He had to go home because of the Covid-19 pandemic and all the restrictions that we were under. All I could do was pray. I knew in my heart that I had to fight with the Word of God. It was important to not get distracted with things like texting and social media because it was important that I kept my mind on the Almighty.

I continued to watch my daughter on a link that was given to us so we could see that she was ok. My husband was checking on us frequently; however, I couldn't breathe without oxygen. I couldn't even lay in the hospital bed, I had to sit up in a chair for comfort. That night my nurse had to call the rapid response team again because my condition was continuing to decline. The team came in and decided that I needed to be rushed to respiratory immediately. I was given a sticky note with the phone number where they were taking my child, and with tears I watched as she went one direction, and I went another.

I was able to quickly take a picture of the note and send it to my husband along with an update on what was happening. One of the last things I said via text was the doctor will call you. I remember them putting me onto the bed in the new room when I got to the respiratory department, they put increased oxygen on my nose, and then I fell straight back onto the bed.

Nine days had passed by the time I had awakened. During that time, I had been on a ventilator, and woke up to a breathing tube, along with my arms strapped down to the bed. I was in ICU with two nurses on duty taking care of me. When my eyes opened that day, the nurse that was beside me was so excited and took her time to tell me what was going on. She then contacted my husband so I could hear his voice. While she was doing that, I looked at the board and saw that it was April 22nd and that so much time had come and gone. I couldn't talk, but it was at that moment that I had to tell the Lord Thank You, because He was still working. He was keeping me, and I knew that He still had more for me to do.

These three words come to my mind often: thankful, grateful, and blessed. Thankful that God's Word is true and a living Word. Thankful that He chose me, and He healed my body! Thankful that He is faithful! Thankful that I can share my story of how good God is! Thankful that The Almighty will put those pieces back together. Thankful that I can still praise and share His goodness with others.

Grateful for everyday that I am blessed. Grateful for praying family and friends. When I was given my cell phone, it was filled with text messages from so friends and family with faith-filled words? That was something I was going to need during my healing process. I could only see people via video because of the pandemic. I was isolated but not along because God was still with me.

Blessed to have so many great prayer warriors that did not wavier in their prayers. Blessed that I was still breathing even though I was still intubated and was off the ventilator. Blessed to be still alive even If I couldn't walk, but I knew that the Almighty was not done yet. I was still in ICU and the physical therapist recommendation was that I be moved to a rehab facility because I couldn't walk, and I still needed help with my speech too. But God!!! Before that transition could happen, I was moved to a room but not on the therapy floor, I was on the floor where new mothers were. I had three days before physical therapy would come back and make the final decision rather to move me to the rehab facility. I had to keep praying and encouraging myself with the Word of God.

With God all things are possible if you believe. Love God with all your heart during the good times and challenging times. When physical therapy came back, I could walk the short distance that they asked me to walk. I was speaking God's word every step, praying that they would put into their report that I wouldn't need to go to the rehab facility.

I saw them as they were having a lengthy discussion in the hallway after they completed my check-up. I kept believing that I would receive good news. That day, they recommended that I stay in the hospital and for me to keep doing my walking in the hallways until the doctors approved for me to be discharged. All the glory belongs to God I was walking little by little, but I was walking and didn't have to go to rehab!!!

They couldn't believe it because they had already decided on where I was going. The caseworker had been in contact with my husband about my transition, but God said no. That evening the nurse that was with me when I had to be rushed to respiratory came to see me. She told me that she couldn't leave me that night and when they got me through those doors, she was praying that I would get better. I had no idea that she was helping push the bed I was on through those hallways.

Jesus looked at them intently and said, "Humanly speaking, it is impossible. But not with God. Everything is possible with God. Mark 10:27 (NLT)

Every step throughout the journey God had people in place working, praying, and believing. I was reminded that this was bigger than me and God chose me to go through this. This was part of His plan for my life, and I am thankful that I am His masterpiece. Have faith that God will do just what He said He would do in your life. Even if it's two, five, or ten years later, keep trusting that He will complete the work that was started in you. God knows the plans that He has for us all and we have been supplied the tools to help us along the way.

Be encouraged and know that you are God's masterpiece. You have been created and chosen by God to live the life He has planned for you. You are valuable and God has done a great thing by creating you. See your uniqueness in Christ through your "Test"imonies. Allow your experiences to help you be more like Him and accept the love that God has for you. Share that love with others so God will continue to get the glory from your life. Don't be ashamed because through these changes and test He is transforming you into a beautiful masterpiece for His use.

I pray that you are encouraged by my testimony and know that God is always taking those pieces and moments molding you for His continued use. Life is precious and it's a gift from God. Keep pressing forward and know He is making all things beautiful in your life. You are God's masterpiece!

Reverend Linda. A. Housden, R.N.

"Servant of God, Lovely Linda"
"God desires a surrendered heart"

*But without faith it is impossible to please him: for
he that cometh to God must believe that He is,
and that His is a rewarder of them that diligently seek Him.*
Hebrews 11:6

Linda A. Housden is a Certified Life Coach, Chief
Community Liaison, for Xcellence Inc., a 17-year Senior
Lead First Responder for the Los Angeles Mayor's Crisis
Response Team, the Public Relations Director for the
company of Ijascode, the one of a kind global, incentivized
digital marketing ecosystem, and co-author of two books,
titled Living God's Best Life, and Living Abundantly.

Email: lindahousden@yahoo.com
Ijascode Webinar: www.ijascode.com/schedule/172
Phone Messages: 818-360-9888

49

I AM GOD'S MASTERPIECE

A lot can happen in a year which can alter your life, teach you to be an overcomer, and find victory and prosperity along the way. This past year, I learned how my being broken needed to be looked at as a gift because it allowed me to recognize the need for my Lord and Savior to make me whole in a way I had never experienced.

On October 3, 2021, I had awakened at 5 a.m. with every intention to work outside and tend to my beautiful rose garden. I had a list of things that I wanted to complete, knowing that my husband and I planned to be in Las Vegas on October 24, 2021, to care for my sister following her double mastectomy surgery scheduled for October 26, 2021. My calendar was full. I had already prearranged for delivery of the supplies needed for my husband's daily wound care and scheduled his dialysis treatment in a Las Vegas facility for three times weekly.

I was checking off my list of "to-dos," so I went out to prune my roses. Little did I know how this day would change things. No sooner when I stepped up on our three-foot high planter to prune the roses, I lost my balance and fell backward landing flat on my back in excruciating pain. I laid there crying for over an hour and screaming for help. My husband, not wearing his hearing aids and sleeping, did not hear my cries for help. Still, as I laid there staring into a pale, blue sky I had no response from neighbors or even the police helicopter that flew overhead. I could wiggle my toes and was grateful, so I began to thank God for the little things.

Finally, my friend, Debbie, was out walking her dog, and heard my cry for help. She came to my gate and immediately called the paramedics who soon arrived to render their assistance. Eight handsome firemen hovered over me. Two, I recognized, and had worked with previously. This is where my story of brokenness began. It is also why I decided to participate in the writing of this amazing book, "From Broken Pieces to Masterpieces."

The paramedics suspected that I had broken my back. They boarded me and transported me to the nearest trauma center. This was the beginning of a journey I had not planned. Little did I know that my attending physician would inform me that I had sustained three compression fractures and would need physical therapy to re-learn how to walk and that I had to use a full body brace for over six months. I couldn't believe this was happening. What was I going to do? I wanted to be done with this. I had a speech to give on October 23, 2021, for my company event where I would be honored as the newest Grand Diamond Affiliate.

Was this a lesson of humility? I was transferred by ambulance from the trauma center to the Country Sheraton Villa Rehabilitation Center in Mission Hills, California, where I began my physical therapy program. I soon made friends with my roommate, Rosa, my walker, my caregivers, my therapists, bedpan, and overhead trapeze bar.

On arrival, I had been immediately evaluated and told what to expect regarding my plan of care. I had already been fitted with my body brace and was scheduled to be on Morphine and Percocet with Zofran to manage my pain level and help with the associated nausea. I intended to push myself to reach every single goal set with my physical therapist. This part wasn't new to me as I was in this facility following my total knee replacement in 2016 and made steady progress. I didn't realize that learning to walk again would be so difficult. Not only was the brace heavy, awkward, and made me feel clumsy, but they told me that it would be necessary for me to put it on by myself within a few days. They medicated me 30 minutes before each therapy session which caused me the inability to focus, much less think about getting discharged by my goal of October 23, 2021, but I was determined to make it.

The first time that I was assisted to sit at the side of the bed, I screamed loudly. I was extremely disappointed that I was only able to take one step. In that moment, my only thought was how I could have prevented my accident. In addition, I thought about how much my husband needed me at home as his caregiver. Fortunately, my husband was able to prepare his meals, as well as drive to his dialysis appointments with a few friends checking in on him. Home health nurses came daily to change Ted's foot bandage. The second day of therapy was just as disappointing, as I was only able to take two steps. The third day, I had a glimmer of hope and progress with eight steps. I made a final peace with God on the third day by thanking him for my progress to come and standing on the promise, "I will walk by faith even when I cannot see" (2 Cor. 5:7 KJV).

Little by little I experienced progress and was able to walk to the door of my hospital room with my roommate, Rosa, became my best cheerleader. Eventually, I was able to walk into the hallway with the aid of a gait belt and my physical therapist. Gout in my left foot set in as a temporary complication hindering my ability to walk easily. I was determined that this wouldn't get in the way of my early planned discharge date of October 20, 2021. I met this goal.

I went home, attended my company of Ijascode event on October 23, 2021, as the honoree and was able to present my speech. I had no time to find a new dress for the occasion, but I found the perfect blue chiffon pant suit at home to cover my body brace well. I was so excited to attend this event that when it was time for me to walk to the front of the room to speak, I recall being handed two microphones. I took both of them in hand as I used my walker to make my way to the front of the room. God used what had just happened to fill the room with his joy prior to my speaking to the attendees. God was faithful and I had accomplished my goal.

On October 24, 2021, the day following the Ijascode event, my sister, Sherri, drove Ted and I to Las Vegas in our car, as planned. In our rush to leave, I misplaced my phone and was without it for a week. It was a mystery but soon it was found at the bottom of my sister's purse without any charge. My sister went through her surgery on October 26, 2021, with her friend Rose and I, by her side. Rose came from Nebraska and helped care for our family for a month. She was able drive Ted to and from his dialysis appointments and help as needed. We became a team of God's recovering children with unquestionable divine favor against all odds. God's favor was indeed the power that propelled us all.

Ted and I decided to return to our home just before Christmas when our friend, Nancy, from Henderson, offered to drive us back to California in our car, since neither of us could drive. On December 26, 2021, we were unable to go to church because Ted felt ill and later that day he fell in the bathroom. I called 911 because I was unable to lift him due to my fractured back. He was taken to the hospital and diagnosed as being dehydrated and having COVID. He was hospitalized until January 15, 2022. I was unable to visit him due to COVID restrictions.

On January 15th, Ted was transferred to the Country Sheraton Villa Rehabilitation Center where he made progress until January 22nd when he was readmitted to the hospital because he developed aspiration pneumonia. Ted remained in the hospital until February 2, 2022, bathed in prayer, hoping that he would again fight the good fight of faith and be able to come home at some point. This never happened. On February 2, 2022, the day after my birthday, I was finally allowed to visit Ted at the hospital. I took a video of us singing "Happy Birthday" together. it is a video that is now dear to my heart.

Later that day, Ted was transferred to a different rehab facility. I expressed to the Discharge Case Management

Team that my desire was for Ted to return to the Country
Sheraton Villa facility. I was not happy with the care at
this current facility. I had difficulty reaching the nurses to
check on Ted's condition and again was not allowed to visit
him due to COVID restrictions. On February 12, 2022,
after three attempts to reach staff regarding my husband's
condition, with no response, I called and requested that
Ted's attending physician return my call. The physician
returned my call when he arrived at the facility. To my
surprise, I was told that Ted had a 102.5 temperature, was
unconscious and was being transferred to the closest ER.

I rushed to the ER and was informed that I couldn't enter
without a negative COVID test. I informed Security of my
husband's condition and told them I wasn't going to stand
there and waste time. At that moment, a staff member
came to the door to observe my bold behavior and reached
out her hand to take my hand and lead me to my husband.
Her only comment to security was, "She's fine, I've got
her." She was the admitting attendant who I had met when
I was admitted with my broken back. God surely gave me
his favor. Once I saw Ted behind the curtain, I grabbed his
hand and said, "Ted, Ted, squeeze my hand if you hear
me." This he did, providing me assurance that he knew that
I was there by his side.

I felt so helpless, and my heart was hurting to see him
unshaven and unconscious. Once again, I asked him loudly
to squeeze my hand and he did. I noticed that the monitor
indicated that his blood pressure was low. At this time,
three nurses entered to turn and reposition Ted. He was in

lots of pain and suffering. I saw that he had developed a large and deep decubitus ulcer. The nurses were cleaning out feces from this huge wound site. My immediate thought was that sepsis had set in. I was overwhelmed with a variety of emotions and remembered two doctors wanted to speak with me. The hospital Chaplain arrived and met with me as I made difficult decisions. Ted was transferred to the oncology floor to be given comfort measures until Jesus would take him home. I was thankful to have our children, Cheri, and Greg with me. He passed away the following evening, February 13, 2022. My favorite nurse, Angel, who admitted Ted, was there with me when Ted died. This was just another provision from God, a nurse named Angel.

After my husband passed away, I noticed a mural outside my husband's hospital room. It read, "You have within you the strength, the patience, and the passion to reach for the stars to change the world." I felt that this was a parting message from my husband. I miss my husband daily. Through my lengthy journey of healing from October until the present, I have often pondered on the faithfulness of God to send those eight firemen. The number eight represents new beginnings, and I was ready for victory, prosperity, and overcoming. This is my heart's desire because I have my eyes set on a life of success, quality leadership, and I'm willing to go great lengths to accomplish what it is that I set out to accomplish.

I encountered one hindrance after another which constantly prevented me from writing my story to be included in this book. This was true even with my posted declarations, periodic check-ins with Dr. A, ongoing prayer, perseverance, and practicing my faith. As the deadline date approached, I thought that I would draw back at one point and block the thought, "I just could not finish, due to added health problems which I personally encountered, and processing the grief associated with the passing of my husband, Ted, on February 13, 2022, the day before Valentine's Day."

Most of one's unbelief centers on the perception of who we think we are. In Christ, it is important to walk out our individual journeys in the spirit of our mind. God is a God of revelation and he revealed to me that he has imparted the gift of motivating others to reach out for whatever seems unreachable. "My grace is sufficient for you, for my power is made perfect in weakness. Therefore, I will boast all the more gladly of my weakness so that the power of Christ may rest upon me (2 Cor. 12:90 KJV).

On August 4, 2022, I was reading the devotional book, "Be Still and Know," by Julie Rayburn. This little book has offered me hope and encouragement at times when I felt that I needed an extra touch from God. I would like to acknowledge God's voice spoken to me on this same day with the scripture verse that I read, "My sheep listen to my voice, I know them, and they follow me." (John 10:27 KJV).

I had experienced God's favor many times over in my life so what exactly were the lessons I needed to learn now, I wondered. Again and again, I was challenged by extreme fatigue, brain fog, severe insomnia, and pain. Generally, I wasn't feeling well and desperately needed rest. Stressors can often interfere with one's performance, but would I allow these to interfere with my performance? I wrote down encouraging Facebook posts for myself and made them personal. For example: "God will finish all that he started in my life; the delay will be turned into a miracle for me! This is a season. God will amaze me with his goodness and favor. I am going to see my prayers answered." He was just beginning to reveal his goodness and favor.

I had an exploratory thyroid/parathyroidectomy procedure done on July 13, 2022, with added minor complications and a trip post op to the emergency room. I could not lift the weight of my head up with the rest of my body without the use of a folded towel. It was unlike anything I had ever seen in my entire nursing career. I practiced self-talk in that situation with these words:

> The light of God surrounds me
> The love of God enfolds me
> The power of God protects me
> The presence of God watches over me
> The mind of God directs me

Wherever I am, the Lord will be my strength and comfort. I renamed my "stressors" to be called "challenged temporary stressors which I know can contribute to performance opportunities." My dear friend, Marcia

Dixon, uses the expression, "Decide and do, it's all up to you." I have a favorite line, too: "Sort and shift," which caused me to push through to enter the completion zone and share my testimony.

I am grateful to my family, friends, mentors, pastors, and prayer partners who accompanied me on this lengthy journey. My appreciation is extended into eternity. "I thank my God upon every remembrance of you." (Phil. 1:3 KJV). Their prayers, good wishes kind deeds, and love provided me the strength to persevere and warmed my heart. I love and appreciate the teachings of Dr. Angella Banks, Xcellence Inc., who teaches that excellence matters, and my friend Devin Schubert, Founder of Legendary Leadership Today, who teaches that authentic leadership starts with the heart and ends with a legacy.

With the help of the Father, I shall live these truths out as I continue in my physical, emotional, and spiritual healing process. Today, I realize that I am much more than a widow. I am a thriving, independent, courageous disciple for Christ who wants my courage and perseverance to matter for others on their individual journeys in life. One must continually search for ways to maintain and improve a positive attitude because I have learned that it is a most priceless possession that works when applied. God makes all things new. What I have realized since the loss of my husband is that I can trust myself. I've survived so much, and I will survive whatever is coming next with the help of God.

Dr. Mary Jo Johnson

Founder of Dayspring Communications, Inc. | Resource Scout

Mary Jo Johnson is the Founder and Director of Dayspring Communications, a 501c3, and she currently serves as the Chief Financial Officer (CFO) of Xcellence, Inc., a global non-profit headquartered in Brownsville, Tennessee. She is also a Paralegal for a local East Bay law firm specializing in asbestos litigation. Dr. Mary Jo is a Licensed Missionary Evangelist through the Church of God in Christ.

Dr. Mary Jo enjoys reading and writing. She mentors students pursuing Spiritual Life Coaching certifications and becoming published Authors through Xcellence Leadership Institute. Dr. Mary Jo holds a Doctor of Education (Ed.D.) degree and is currently drafting her dissertation for a Doctor of Philosophy (Ph.D.) in Biblical Studies.

Visit our website: www.dayspringcommunication.org

Email: dayspgcom2014@gmail.com | Telephone: 510-318-1374

I AM GOD'S MASTERPIECE

God takes our brokenness and makes something beautiful of it. Brokenness was formerly the story of my life. At the age of twelve, I lost my earthly father to gun violence. Losing my father at the age of twelve was a devastating experience. My battle with depression began after my father's death. I was so lonely and sad. We had a close father/daughter bond. That bond was irrevocably broken.

My mother worked hard to keep our family together and to ensure our needs were met. It was not until I became an adult that I thought about how my father's death must have impacted her. I am sure she had her own emotions to deal with, handling them the best way she could. Growing up I never learned about therapy and the importance of guarding one's mental health. I knew of sadness, devastation, and suffering loss. As I grew older, I looked for love in the wrong places. I never found love in any of those places; I remember abuse and pretention. I seemed to gravitate toward it. I was attracted to someone who did not want me but didn't want anyone else to have me.

King Solomon, the wisest man to have lived, wrote, "Remember now thy creator in the days of thy youth…" My days as a youth were dark and dreary. While in college I went home for the weekend. I attended my church. My pastor preached on "spiritual inventory". That sermon was life changing. The impact was immediate.

As a child, my sainted grandmother taught us about holiness and how God wanted us to live. As a child, it did not register. As I matured, it made sense. My uncle translated what my grandmother was telling us. He used words and analogies I could understand. As I began to take "spiritual inventory," I immediately put his words into practice. He taught us how to carry ourselves as young adults. My grandmother gave us scripture; my uncle taught us practicality. I remember their teaching even today. When God has his hands on our lives, the enemy tries to thwart God's plan by blinding us to the truth. I often heard preachers and elders point me out in church telling me I was gifted. I recall the gospel pricking my heart at age nine. I gave my heart to God and was baptized.

I had a personal quest for God. I loved God and would pray for his deliverance in my life. I needed God's saving grace, something I had not yet learned or heard about. The adage "Birds of a feather flock together," held plenty truth until I learned better. Always wanting to be in the know and never understanding the truth of God's love was my reality. I enjoyed hanging out with my cousins and the people I was growing up with. I felt a need for validation; I needed to know my life mattered. We come to know how much we matter when we yield ourselves to God.

Sadly, I was looking at my natural life. God saw my spirit and his plan for my salvation. The scripture tells us God will not despise a broken spirit and a contrite heart. The sermon on spiritual inventory changed my life. Almost out of college by then, I felt change was coming. Still feeling lonely and depressed, I began my search for God. I knew this would be my change.

I remember when the Holy Ghost came upon me in my senior year of college. Jesus spoke to my heart and said, "Come out from amongst them." Letting go of the world was a huge ordeal. Satan did not want this sinner to get away. Thank God I was able to get out of his grip.

I recommitted my life to Christ. I still had my struggles with the world. The journey was not easy, but it has been worth it. I remember my call to ministry. I now endeavor to make that calling and election sure.

God takes broken pieces and make masterpieces. I was a broken vessel that the potter put together. He took the broken pieces of my life and made me new. He gave me value and worth by transforming me into his image and likeness. Christ took away the spirit of heaviness and replaced it with the garment of praise. He took the sadness and depression and gave me joy and a renewed mind. Only God can take a troubled soul and cause it to be a designer's original. Today my life is full of peace. Despite health challenges, I rest in God's goodness. He is working in mysterious ways, his wonders to perform.

Blessings to almighty God for snatching my life out of the hands of the enemy. He gave me a future and a hope. I praise God for not giving up on me. I almost gave up on myself. I thank God for speaking to my heart in 1986 telling me that he was going to take everything I have been through and cause it to be a blessing to people. A year before that he told me he was giving me the ministry of exhortation. God took the broken pieces of my life and made a masterpiece, a woman of God. He made me one of a kind; everyone who comes to Christ and makes him Lord, becomes one of a kind, a masterpiece, a designer's original. We have a one-of-a-kind love for each other. No good thing has he withheld. I can come boldly before the throne of grace to obtain mercy in a time of need.

The scripture tells me that I can seek God and I will find him when I search for him with my whole heart. I became hungry for a relationship with God. When I came to know that God loves me, I also came to realize the great things he does for his children. God's love is rooted in truth. I had to learn the truth about God's love and forgiveness. I had to learn to forgive myself for the mistakes I made in the past. I had to forgive myself for being disobedient to my mother who always tried to tell me the truth. I learned to embrace the truth of God's grace. I did not know the truth; I was walking in error until I fully surrendered to Christ, until I searched for him with my whole heart.

My mandate is to share the good news. Jesus saves; he heals; and he forgives. None of us are beyond his saving grace. Christ paid for our redemption on Calvary. The work was finished on the cross. We can walk in victory. I live to bring glory to my savior by helping others. I am his masterpiece.

Ministry has been more than preaching for me although I do a bit of that too. I was called to servant leadership. I have been blessed to assist in hospital and convalescent ministry, prison visitation, homeless care, and crisis pregnancy counseling. I was granted the opportunity to do a lot of pastoral counseling and care. In fact, I have been dubbed a pastor by many. What it has been for me is the call to serve others. I especially engage in it now. It allows me to use the ministry of exhortation.

I was called to feed God's sheep. For the longest I did not understand what this meant although I have known since elementary school that I was called to teach. I work with individuals on all levels to help them excel and achieve their academic and career goals. This is fulfilling and rewarding. I also teach in the church, Sunday School, Bible study, and in workshops. This is a huge part of my role as a servant leader.

Life for me in this season is about walking in love and loving others as God does. I am intentional about my relationships. I endeavor to be focused and present. I don't find it necessary to say I love you so much as I do to show I love you. Love is an action word, a verb. As it is said, I would rather see a good sermon than to hear one. Besides, a person knows when I genuinely care about them and when I am just paying lip service. I say this because I know who is in my corner and who is not. I trust others will know when I am in their corner also.

This topic gave me an opportunity to reflect. I realize how much I have grown and matured spiritually since I started my journey. I reflect on how important my family and our relationships are to me. I also reflected on how God called me to listen and to be there for others. When I pray for

God's guidance and direction for the people he wants me to witness to each day, I realize that is everyone I encounter. If it is just a smile or a pleasant hello, I am called to show the love of Christ. This is one broken piece turned masterpiece that must be about her father's business.

Amy Ouellette

Founder of Footprints to Health Ministries (coming soon); which will be a faith-based, holistic, Spa/Wellness Retreat and Community Learning Center, an Alumni of The Institute for Integrative Nutrition Health Coaching School, and a Certified Integrative Nutrition Health Coach. Amy is trustworthy, passionate HOPE advocate, with high integrity ready to serve you and help you tackle and achieve your desired health goals.

Raised in a Christ-follower home, she is the oldest of 5 children. Amy is single and a divorced mom of 2 amazing children. She enjoys deepening her relationship with the Lord every day, as He grows her and molds her for His purpose and glory.

Email: coachamy@footprintstohealth.org

I AM GOD'S MASTERPIECE

Well, here it is! My story for God's glory! I can still remember it like it was yesterday. It was January 2011. My tall, dark, and handsome Christian husband of six and a half years graduated from Law school. He passed the BAR exam and was recently sworn in as an attorney. A short time after, there was a beautifully written, locally published news article about him being a new attorney, ready to serve our local community. The article stated how he married the love of his life - me. He loved his family, loved being a dad, was happy to be an attorney, etc. I later learned that he was the one who wrote his own article.

Soon we were expecting our second child. A sweet, heaven-sent baby girl this time. I felt larger than an elephant, with a huge belly the size of a basketball. I was waddling more like a penguin each day, or so it seemed that way anyway. Our firstborn son was three years old, all excited, looking forward to his new baby sister's arrival. I was home now on a month early of maternity leave, per my doctors' orders, due to borderline preeclampsia concerns and increasing fatigue. One day, I was paying some of our bills. I was the one who made sure our bills got paid. One of our utility e-bills had to be paid by a certain time that day, but I needed access to my husband's personal email account to pay it. We hadn't yet made the necessary changes to have the e-bill sent to my email account.

I was having more pregnancy brain that day and couldn't seem to remember his email password, so I called him at work. We talked for a few minutes, and I explained to him that I needed to pay one of our utility bills but couldn't remember his email password. So, I asked him for the password, which sounded like the right one, but he seemed a little hesitant to give it to me at first. I didn't think much about his hesitation. I was tired and just wanted to get the bills paid, so I could go rest in bed and relax more.

He went on to say he wasn't sure if the email password he gave me was the correct one and told me not to worry about trying to access it until he got home a little later that night. Again, not thinking much about his hesitation, I explained to him that the bill was due by a certain time that day and it also had our account number on it, which I needed in order to pay it, so he said OK. We finished our conversation and ended the call. I proceeded to attempt his email password, and it was successful. I was in! Thank God, because I was already stressing out about other things, in preparation for our daughter's upcoming birth.

As I was scrolling through all of his emails, mostly junk emails - gotta love it, I hadn't yet come across the e-bill I was looking for, so I kept scrolling. Then, suddenly I saw something that immediately caught my eye. I stopped scrolling and couldn't believe what I was seeing! An email from my youngest brother's ex-girlfriend to my husband! She and I became friends when her and my youngest brother were dating a few years prior. She had also babysat our son for us at times. What? No way!! What was this all about? How could this be?

I had to calm my nerves down and remind myself to breathe! Just breathe! I cried out, "God help me!" Trying my best to give all of this the benefit of a doubt, I opened the email from her. My heart was pounding, my anxiety

69

was through the roof, my stomach was tight in knots, and my breathing quickly became shallow, as I had a mix of emotions running through my mind. The email read something like this - "I am so excited to meet up with you soon at Starbucks…it's been so long since I've seen you…I'm looking forward to catching up more with you…" I began to tear up, then bawled my eyes out! My hormones were already on screech with the pregnancy.

I was beside myself! There I was eight months pregnant with our second child. I thought we were happily married! I thought I was a good wife overall. Yeah, there were many times I was tired and didn't feel like being intimate. I mostly supported us while he was attending college and law school. I was working to help provide for our little family. I did most of the housework, wrote him little love notes at times, made many of our meals, made sure our son was loved on and happy. The list of thoughts going through my mind went on and on, as you could just imagine.

So…I called him back at his office and held my composure emotionally as much as possible until he got on the line. He answered and I told him I couldn't believe an email I just came across. I was beside myself. I was crying as I was asking him lots of questions. "Why did you meet with her at Starbucks? I am eight months pregnant with our daughter right now! Did you touch her? Did you kiss her? Did you hug her?" His reply after each question was "Nooo, Amy" in a deeper, more stern voice than I was familiar with.

He told me there was nothing I needed to worry about and that it was just a casual conversation over coffee. I told him either way, he should have discussed it with me first, instead of going behind my back like that. We were married! He reassured me there was nothing for me to worry about and then went on to tell me he had to finish up some things at the office and would be home in a little bit. He also was going to have to bring work home with him for an upcoming case he had.

It was now February 2011, and I gave birth to our beautiful baby girl. Now we had two most perfect, heaven-sent children from God above! They both brought so much joy to our lives! When our daughter was about two months old, I began experiencing vertigo episodes, increased fatigue, throbbing pains throughout my entire body, along with some other issues. I began to pay closer attention to my symptoms and when they were occurring more or increasing. Shortly after, I was approached by a friend at our church. She was the church Treasurer and asked if I would consider replacing her position. I thought about it, trained for the position and shortly after, became church Treasurer.

As life continued, my Treasurer duties became more demanding, and I was easily spending about 10-15 hours a week. About eight months later, my husband told me he had been thinking for a while that I should consider having someone else take over as Treasurer. He gave some good reasons why, but primarily because it was taking up family time.

71

I began praying more for God to draw my husband and I closer to Him and one another. We had our disagreements here and there, but nothing that seemed alarming. Amongst all of this, we did marital counseling for about six months with an Elder and his wife from our church at the time. It was addressed that he shouldn't have gone out to coffee with another woman behind my back, because we were married. He just seemed to chuckle about it, but then apologized to me about it.

In 2012, I began to see a new primary care physician to mainly address chronic fatigue, vertigo episodes along with some newer symptoms I was having with tingling and numbness in my extremities. I just knew that as a mom in her early 30's, I shouldn't be feeling the way I was, and drinking at least two cups of coffee a day just wasn't helping my energy levels. I requested Lyme testing, but my PCP refused and ordered blood work to check for other things.

My blood results showed high inflammatory markers and other abnormal results, so he referred me to a Rheumatologist. That April I saw the Rheumatologist and had more in-depth blood work done. I hadn't heard anything back from them many months after, so I assumed no news was good news. I was busy with life and motherhood in general. Then one day as I was talking with one of my co-workers, I thought I should contact my Rheumatologist. I quickly learned that my results couldn't be given over the phone, and I had to wait a few more days to be seen.

Waiting those next few days were awful! I had no idea what to think, and my anxieties were increasingly high, as you can just imagine. Come to find out, someone was supposed to follow up with me about my results and schedule an appointment, but it fell through the cracks. My results proved I had a very active auto-immune condition. My body was severely attacking itself! There I was at almost age 32, mom of two, being diagnosed with Schogren's Syndrome and Chronic Fatigue Syndrome.

It was now November 2012, and I was told I'd need to take a prescription the remainder of my life. My anxieties increased more, as well as frustration and feeling angry, because no one followed up with me. I was also mad at myself for not calling their office sooner, but life just happened, and I just pushed my symptoms aside. Soon after starting the prescription, they prescribed me, I had to stop it, because I was experiencing a side effect from it with full body itching. It wasn't pleasant and I became more frustrated! I was getting tired of being told the same old things, with no positive results on my health journey.

My anxieties increased about the whole situation, and I began to feel trapped inside my body. I was a mom of two young children, now at ages five and almost three. I needed to be functioning better so I could be a better wife and a better mom to our kids. So, I began to pray more and more each day, which did help calm my fears a bit. God was teaching me patience and to give it all over to Him. Not long after, I changed my Primary Care Physician. I also started seeing a Christian Chiropractor and had a new patient appointment scheduled with a Naturopathic Doctor as well.

In May 2013, after many visits to the Neurologist, my MRI results came back normal, he expressed his concerns to me about my weight loss and made some suggestions. He put me on a six month recall and told me to call if my symptoms got worse. He then proceeded to ask me if there was anything else he could do for me, that maybe my other providers hadn't done for me yet. I couldn't believe it! He literally read my mind! I was quickly learning how to be my own advocate for my health. I knew how I was supposed to be feeling. After all, he was highly known as a top Neurologist for my local area. So, with a relieving, grateful smile on my face, I asked him to order a Lyme test for me. He said he didn't think I had Lyme but followed through with my request and ordered an expedited Western Blot test, which is a little more in depth than the basic Elisa test. After my appointment that day, I went straight to the lab and had my blood drawn. The following evening, he called me from his private line saying he was quite surprised, but I did in fact test positive for Lyme.

Praise God, I was finally getting more answers! So, we had to seek more natural ways to treat the Lyme. I took a holistic adrenal fatigue tincture from my Naturopath and gradually made more dietary changes. I went gluten free, mostly dairy free, and cut back on my weaknesses of coffee and chocolate. I also learned I wasn't getting in nearly enough of my daily water intake, which should be at least half of our body weight in ounces daily. Months went by and I seemed to be making some progress. Every now and then, my husband would ask me how my appointments were going, and he'd casually mention that I looked like I was getting better. Little did I know what was about to come at me next.

Fast forward to New Year's Eve 2013. We had a small New Year's Eve party at our place with family and close friends from church. Everyone was having a great time! As New Year's Day 2014 approached, we all hugged and wished one another a Happy New Year, and everyone left. After checking on our children, I climbed in bed after a busy, but fun evening. I then noticed my husband come to the threshold of our bedroom. He said he had something to tell me. I was so tired and just wanted to get to bed. I asked him to please hurry up and tell me, because I was exhausted and needed to get some sleep, before the kids woke up early that morning.

He then said some of the most dreaded words, "I want a divorce." I sat up in bed. I was completely shocked! "What? What do you mean you want a divorce? I thought you didn't believe in divorce! What is going on? We have two young children together! Are you kidding me, I asked?" The questions kept coming and the tears began to flow down my face. He then said he had been thinking about it for a while, we did counseling, but I hadn't changed much for his liking. He said he thought I was a hopeless romantic and I was a lot like a family member of mine in a negative way. He also mentioned he didn't want our young children to know about it. I reminded him that a marriage takes two people, not just one and told him I would not keep this news from our children and have them blind-sighted too.

I was so hurt and confused! I cried out to God that night, questioning his goodness, held on to hope as much as I could, and fell asleep crying and praying. I had no idea what to think and my spirit felt heavy and crushed! Depression started creeping in, so I began reading the Bible more, and praying to God more. Soon after, I began to notice the time 9:11, morning or afternoon or both just about every day, no matter where I was. I wasn't sure if I should take that as a good or a bad thing. I know God works in numbers and I didn't know yet what he was trying to tell me. I also ordered a Life Recovery Bible for myself, to help me more through this painful, devastating chapter in my life. I had many other Bibles, but this one really spoke to me for my given circumstances.

A few months went by and oddly enough, things seemed to be fine. We began to meet with our pastor. Family and friends from church talked with us on separate occasions. We were still living in our home together, sleeping in the same bed, and surprisingly, still intimate with each other. There were times he would come on to me, compliment me on how nice I looked, etc. I was being led to believe there was hope for our marriage. Then one early evening, he randomly handed me a stapled, legal document. He was serving me the divorce papers in our very own living room. I couldn't believe it, and I told him how hurt and confused I was.

I tried talking with him more, but it was like I was talking to a brick wall. He already had his mind made up and apparently for a while.

It was craziness! There were evenings I would come home, just bawling my eyes out and he would be there, and not show empathy for me. It was like he didn't know how to handle my emotions. Sometimes he would even smirk while I cried, which baffled my mind and hurt me even more. It was all very nerve-racking. I felt lost, confused, abandoned, and misunderstood.

As time went on, he and I both had to attend a co-parenting class ordered by the judge. It was helpful, and as the class finished, one of the lawyers said to feel free to ask her any other questions after the class. After the lawyer was done talking with a few others, I introduced myself to her and gave her a summarized version of my situation and told her I was a woman of faith in God. In our conversation, I learned that she was also a woman of faith in God. I shared with her that for a while now, I had been seeing the time 9:11 and didn't know if it was a good thing or a bad thing that God was trying to tell me. She encouraged me to look at it as a positive thing and to search the Scriptures that may be applicable to my situation with those numbers.

I told her how much I appreciated her input and thanked her. I hadn't thought of that myself. She reminded me to give myself grace. I was going through a lot and there's only so much that the body and mind can handle during traumatic events. Oh my gosh, she was so right! God used her to show me I needed to give myself more grace. I went home that day and dug right into my Life recovery Bible. It was through my searching that I came across Psalms 91:11 which reads, "For he will order his angels to protect you wherever you go." (NLT version). I felt God's peace come over me and I was so blessed by it! From then on, it became one of my life verses.

I continued to pray more for God's wisdom and guidance in all aspects of my life. Soon after, it came to mind that I needed to see a Lyme specialist. I strongly felt like it was God guiding me. So, I started seeing a Lyme doctor in September 2014, and he turned out to be a huge help with more answers along my journey. With more detailed blood work that thankfully was mostly covered by insurance, we discovered that I had chronic Lyme, four coinfections/strains of Lyme and a gene mutation, which makes it difficult for my body to detox. He educated me on the importance of proper liver function, proper vitamin D, methylated B vitamins and magnesium levels as well. What he was telling me made so much sense to me.

77

Then, one Monday morning in October 2014, I arrived at work, got settled in, and as I was answering an incoming call, my manager walked over and quietly mentioned she'd like to see me in the office once I was done with the call.

So, I finished the call, walked down to the office and upon entering, the Dentist welcomed me in to have a seat as he always had in the past and the manager closed the door as I sat down. Ohh, this wasn't good! The Dentist starts saying how he knew I have a lot going on with my divorce and my health, and he hated to do this to me, but they received some recent patient complaints about me, so they decided they had to let me go. They both apologized and wished me the best as I began to tear up. As our quick meeting ended, I gathered my personal items at the front reception area, said goodbye to one of my co-workers who was also shocked.

To some extent, I started to feel like a female version of Job in the Bible. My whole world was crashing to pieces all around me! But GOD reminded me in His word that He promises us a FUTURE and a HOPE! (Jeremiah 29:11). About a month later, in November 2014, my kids and I were able to move in at my parents' place. I also learned from the Unemployment office that my former employer was denying paying for unemployment, so I had to start the process of disputing that as well. It was now 7 months into the divorce process, and my health was getting worse by the minute it seemed. I was at the point where I was getting very concerned if I would even be able to handle caring for our children by myself.

About a week after the divorce finalized, I was in town with my youngest brother who was getting groceries done for me. Before we headed back home, he asked me if I needed to get any mail at my former home before we headed back home. As my ex-husband answered the door, he said he wasn't expecting me. I told him I had texted him about me picking up my mail. It was a little dark, but I then quickly noticed, straight ahead of me, a shadow of a person trying to quietly run from my former living room into our former bedroom. I asked him who was there, and he said it wasn't my business. Well, as you can imagine, I needed to know, so I walked past him as I slowly approached my former bedroom. Behind the bedroom door, there she was! My youngest brother's ex-girlfriend!

As I found her with her head down, hiding behind the bedroom door, she looked up and said, "Amy, it's not what you think it is." I told her I didn't believe her and how dare she even be there after not even a week after the divorce finalizing. Surprisingly, as angry and hurt as I was, I didn't swear, but I did yell at her. I will spare the rest of the details, but I was beside myself!

A quick side note, at the time I write this, my ex-husband recently got engaged to my youngest brother's ex-girlfriend. Even though I have moved on, the news was a hard gulp for me to swallow, as the pain tries to creep back up and sneak itself back in. Through it all, God has remained faithful and has shown me the importance and necessity of forgiveness, and to look inwardly, reflect, and make sure there's no bitterness remaining or unforgiveness.

Not long after, I applied for Disability, as I was still unable to drive or work. I heard how difficult it was to get approved first try, but I put those things aside, prayed about it, and kept the faith as much as I could. Before we mailed my disability application, I asked my dad to pray over it, as my parents and I all put our hands over the large envelope.

Things took time, but then one summer day in 2016, I got a call from Social Security Administration. I was approved for SSDI! Hallelujah! About 6 months later, my kids and I were able to move in to our own little 2-bedroom apartment. I was so grateful and praised God for His help and goodness

Through my trials and tribulations, God showed me how I could help others on their health journey too. In December 2019, I finally took the leap out of my comfort zone and enrolled as a health coach student at the Institute for Integrative Nutrition, and a little over a year later, after much hard work and getting in my accredited hours, I was officially a Certified Integrative Nutrition Health Coach.

Through this healing journey, God has gently shown me and reminded me that we, as God's children, are commanded to "forgive as Christ forgave us." (Col. 3:13). God continues to grow me and lead me to very humbling experiences, where I have no other choice but to trust and rely on Him to take care of my children and me.

To this day, I still see the time 9:11 and more recently began seeing the time 11:11. Whenever I have a hint of worry creep in, I have divine moments where I will suddenly hear the song "Sparrow" by Cory Asbury playing on the Christian radio station. He reminds me that He provides for the birds and even we are more valuable than they are. (Matt. 6:26). So, no matter what it is that you have gone through or may be going through now, remember God has it!

As I close this out, I had to share quickly with you, a huge vision the Lord downloaded to me more recently after asking him a simple question if he wanted me to do something more besides health coaching. He immediately dropped in my spirit "a faith-based Spa/Wellness (Retreat and Learning) Center. I couldn't believe it and was blown away. After much conversation with the Lord as to "Why me?" He has shown me how he has chosen me, and this is so much grander than I ever planned or anticipated. I requested to the Lord shortly after for this "Spa/Wellness Center" to be in my hometown because we greatly need this in our community and globally as well.

About one week later I strongly felt God show me the property for Footprints to Health Ministries, as I was bringing my son home from school. It has since turned into greater things, with plans of an Air BNB, camping, special events venue, evening bonfire worship under the stars, floral and lavender gardens, along with health coaching services, a wellness shop and much more! Overall, a one-stop place for your much needed self-care needs! I am not sure what the finished mission will look like, but I know one thing for sure, it's all for God's glory - to help grow His kingdom.

So friend, remember, your trials and tribulations in life can turn into your testimony, and help deliver incredible amounts of hope and joy to the world. You are God's chosen royalty and are here NOW, "for such a time as this!" (Esther 4:14). "Make your life a masterpiece; imagine no limitations on what you can be, have or do." - Brian Tracy. There is only ONE YOU, and you are God's Masterpiece! Shine on my friend! Cast out the enemy's schemes in Jesus' mighty name and remind the enemy that you are a child of the living, Most High God, and He can redeem anything! After all, God is amazing at redemption too, isn't He? Much love to you! I pray this blessed your heart in some way, in Jesus' name, AMEN!

Anika K. Hamilton-Singleton

Poet, Spoken Word Artist, and Author of "Urban Eyes Flames of My Time", a book of Poetry

Anika is also a Transformational, Motivational and Inspirational Speaker who uses her life experiences to help others heal, coaching them to see how they can become the best version of themselves. She pricks the heart, invokes change, and offers a blueprint of how to overcome the facets of life. A woman of today's time, for today's time.

Born and raised in Oakland CA, she is Wife Mother and Entrepreneur. She holds an MFA in Writing and Consciousness from New College of California, San Francisco, and a B.S. in Criminal Justice Administration from San Jose State University.

Email: Anikakenyatta@gmail.com | Phone: 510-978-9772

I AM GOD'S MASTERPIECE

Have you ever asked for something, got it, and then were unappreciative of it? Because when it was presented to you it really wasn't the version you wanted, causing you to be upset, even angry? So much that you despised the person who gave it to you and how they delivered it to you. That's how I felt when I met my sister.

I was seventeen years old in my last year of high school when I met my older sister. My father's daughter by another woman whom I knew nothing about. To make matters worse she was born between my brother and I who shared the same mother and father.

Now just imagine, at school, between classes, being handed a note that read "I think you are my sister please call me." Here I was living my life and the only thing on my mind at that moment was Senior activities and graduation day. But no, here I was overwhelmed with anxiety of a daunting discovery that came a little too late for my enjoyment by way of a note from a friend. So, my response was one of resentment, annoyance, and non-acceptance after I read the note. I was devasted and went to my mother in tears about what I had found out. To my surprise my mother wasn't surprised. She knew about her and encouraged me to get to know my sister.

After speaking with my mother and the initial shock wore off me having a sister, I reached out and called the number on the note. Although I had agreed to meet with her, I was still apprehensive, skeptical, and nervous. My sister, on the other hand was excited, talkative, and anticipated the union. I didn't have a clue how I was supposed to feel about a sister I didn't grow up with. I felt as though in order to be sisters we had to have shared childhood memories, and for us we had none. My brothers and sisters we grew up together and held memories in common. They knew my likes and dislikes, my fears, and joys. We shared rooms, beds, and secrets. We had fights and were made to make up and taught to love each other because we were sisters and brothers. We were taught to look out for each other. Our bond was formed a long time ago. And now after years of wanting another sister, here she was, and instead of being happy about it, I was angry and annoyed.

My sister was all smiles when we met however, I half-heartedly smiled as I was unsure of what I was supposed to say or what she expected. She must have felt my apprehension because she quickly assured me, she just wanted to get to know me and understood it wasn't easy for me. She explained how she had been searching for my brother and I for some time and just wanted to get to know us. We started with small talk with her leading the conversation. I responded and that's how things went for the first couple of encounters. I found out we were both in our senior year of high school just at different schools, and we knew many of the same people.

Eventually, over the course of our senior year, my heart softened, and we began to talk more and even hung out from time to time. My sister was the epitome of a big sister, overprotective, crazy, and loving all at the same time. I was surprised to find out we held much of the same feelings towards our father and that drew us even closer. Neither had a relationship with him other than knowing he was our father. We both had other siblings and we both got to know them as well. We started going to see our great grandmother together, spending time with our father's side of the family. Oddly as it was, we didn't run into our father, the connection that made us sisters and the reason we didn't grow up together.

Forging a relationship over the years wasn't easy. We spent our early twenties in and out of each other's lives. Our children did know each other, and we would periodically drop by each other's homes, laugh, and catch up on life. We would go months without seeing each other and then have a great weekend of sister bliss. However, it was in my mid-twenties when I was going thru some of the most devasting times in my life we reconnected on a much deeper level. The murder of my brother, death of my mother, and the passing of my stepfather brought our relationship closer, and God began to open my eyes to the blessing I had in my sister. Her strength and love of steadfastness broke down walls that I had around me and helped me open my heart at a time when I was shutting down to the world.

It was during these times she became more than just my father's other daughter. She became my friend; someone I could confide in, and someone I knew had my back. She was not just my blood sister. I began to realize how special and important she was to my life. My sister had given me unconditional love even in the days I didn't want her as a sister.

I realized I was shifting my feelings of hurt onto another. We found each other in our teens but we both held scars from our childhood of an absent father. She chose to search out and heal her brokenness. I on the other hand, didn't want to have anything to do with her. She was willing to pull the scab off in search of finding her brother and sister. I felt like I was forced to pick at a scab that wasn't bothering me, and as it was uncovered, it caused me to bleed with resentment.

85

As I reflect on our relationship, my sister didn't deserve to be treated the way I treated her. I remember a time when I cried for a sister and then when I got what I wanted I mishandled her. It didn't come how I expected, and I didn't like how the news was delivered. I didn't realize then, what I do now. Nor did I have the capacity to understand and comprehend what my mother was trying to get me to understand. "It wasn't my sister's fault neither was it mine, sometimes it's just the way life is handed to us," My sister was just searching for a part of her that she knew was missing. My resentment was misplaced because I felt as if life had misrepresented itself. I felt ashamed as I got older about the way I acted. I had to come to terms with my past feelings and eventually be woman enough to ask for my sister's forgiveness. Thankfully she understood and was patient with me when she could of easily have walked away.

My beliefs have since changed. It doesn't take a lifetime to create memories. You just have to be open to making them. Today I can't imagine my life without my sister, and it didn't take knowing her from childhood to create the unbreakable bond we have today. It did take me not letting what happen then dictate what we have now. God has a way of giving you back what you thought was time wasted. It's crazy, we often have those silly giggly moments that I thought sisters could only experience as little children.

I now understand adult decisions are not children's burdens to bear. Sometimes children are forced to wear and bear the scars of adult decisions and transgressions. However, it doesn't have to define nor control who we are and what we will become as an adult. It's true, time can heal all wounds but then there are incidences when time is not on our side and circumstances don't permit. In my situation, I was blessed to have time on my side despite the years I wasted fighting not to come to terms with my reality. It was time, love, and acceptance of the fact that I couldn't change the past, but I did have control of how things stood in the moment and how I wished or want my future to be.

I had to make the choice, I could hold on to what I wanted to stay the same, even though I knew it would never be; or I could let go and embrace the newness of life that was filled with the one thing many others long for and that is the unconditional love of a sister.

I realized the assignment was bigger than me. My sister and I were breaking a generational curse before it could be established. I wanted my children, nieces, and nephews to grow up knowing me, and each other. I wasn't a secret to my nieces and nephews and when and if they needed me, I would be there.

Holding on to unresolved hurt had already cost me time with my sister. I was an example of the phrase, "hurt people hurt people." I had to first acknowledge the hurt, sit with it, digest it, wrestle with it, and then decide. I could let it consume my heart and continue to live broken and in pieces or I could open my heart and release the hurt and usher in the possibilities.

Yes, it was uncomfortable. On the other side of uncomfortable is fear and discomfort. It makes you question and doubt because you don't know what's on the other side; but isn't that the definition of faith? "The substance of things hoped for, the evidence of things not seen (Hebrews 11:1 KJV). On the other side I had to go if I wanted to grow. I am thankful I did because I was pleasantly surprised. There was light at the end of a dark tunnel.

Sometimes we get so caught up in the "how come" that we don't see the blessing or the gift in the "how about." Well, "how about" God was working through our relationship to bring the support and comfort that I didn't even know I was in search of. Here I was angry by the "how come." "How come" she popped up in my life, I didn't see it was in perfect timing?

God had positioned things in His time at the right time. God had sent me an anchor in my sister at the darkest most difficult times in my life. Time neither of us knew was coming but when it came my big sister was right there and hasn't left my side since. Her presence and love got me through. We found a gift in each other.

I have been taught many lessons in life and some of the best beneficial ones have come from personal experience. As the elders in my family would say, "bought sense". One being, when you are afforded the opportunity in life to right a wrong, take advantage of God's grace that He gives you through acceptance, forgiveness and being forgiven. That scab that I spoke of has completely healed now. It had to be scrapped off to get me to the point where the bleeding could stop forever. I am learning to let go of the things I cannot control, enjoy the people who God has placed in my life to love me, and the time God has granted me. Many of us have had the same experience but weren't granted the time. Time doesn't wait until you get it together. Time is of the essence. And if time is not met, it becomes a missed opportunity, which may cause you to miss out on what could be the biggest blessing of your life.

Learn to appreciate the gift, even when it doesn't come in a neat and nicely wrapped package. Often, the best gifts come by of a beaten path. Sometimes in ugly wrapping paper. But if you refuse to open it after it makes its way and because of the way it's handed or delivered to you, you'll never enjoy the gift. In my case, my gift was my sister. The delivery wasn't pretty, in fact it crushed me, but when I finally decided to open it, the gift was filled with love, sisterhood and a forever friend.

Kimberly Ivory Taylor

Founder and Owner of PURSUE KIM LLC &

Vision Explosion K.I.M, Your Visionologist

Kimberly Ivory Taylor assist visionaries that connect with her who are first time published authors or existing authors wanting to monetize their books to the max. She offers vision explosion sessions were there are practical actions taken to explore all opportunities and resources for visionaries.

Kimberly has successfully hosted and served selflessly to the community and worldwide through her events, products & services. It's More Than an Experience, It's a Shift!

https://linktr.ee/pursuekim | info@pursuekim.com

I AM GOD'S MASTERPIECE

From Broken Pieces to a Masterpiece is definitely a great way to describe the process of life I have experienced. It has allowed me to recognize that things do not have to stay the same. Change can and will come when you really have the desire for it and get tired of being tired, then a shift is on its way. Are you ready is the question you must ask yourself? Hold on, the ride is a little bumpy, is what I wish someone would have told me.

When you hear the words, "What you don't know can kill you," do you believe them? I heard those words and never really looked at how it would apply to my own life. I was broken into many pieces in many different areas. I had gone many years not realizing I was operating from a broken state. I was comfortable operating and existing in what I know now was disfunction. Disfunction was not easily recognized because everyone around me was operating the same way. Everyone at work, my friends and family. One day you will walk smack into that brick wall and the light bulb will go off. That is what happened to me one day when I got revelation of some things happening in my life.

Let's go back to my childhood where it all started. As a child, I had experienced trauma of being sexually abused by a family member who was a minor themself. Every time this family member was around, I would feel so weird, shaking from the inside, not able to move. I would wonder can anyone else see me shaking or looking confused? I really couldn't explain what was happening in those moments back then, now I realize I was experiencing the trauma all over again, as if it was going to happen right there in front of everyone.

It was almost like I wanted to scream get away or why are you here, and nothing would come out. I would speak to that family member, and even in that, it was a halfway hello. This was not a onetime situation; I remember it taking place many times. I was very young, under 10 years old. I don't remember all the details, but some situations stayed in my memory being rehearsed like it was yesterday. Those times kept playing over and over and over and over in my mind, which made it hard to just remove it from my memory. I grew up feeling different and odd from other people. I always associated how I did things with what had happened to me as a child. It always crosses my mind at family gatherings, "Do they know what happened to me?" I had never spoken about it to anyone at that time in my life.

As a child you look for protection, a covering, and someone you can go to for help. I felt I never had that. I grew up not understanding how to explain how I was really feeling about things. I remember being a child that wouldn't talk around a lot of people, I would just observe. As I got older, I was determined to say whatever I wanted, however I wanted, and I wasn't going to allow anyone or anything to shut me up.

That plan didn't work out well, it was just another part of my broken pieces that the enemy knew, and he used it very well against me to kill and destroy people with my words. I was going to have the last word and hurt your feelings in the process. I was not a person who used curse words, but my combination was deadly, I would try to kill your soul with words. Even if the other person stopped talking, I just kept on going until I was satisfied. I really felt like, if you take the time to push me to a place to get angry, then you are asking for it the way it will come out. Those moments were terrible, I was like a raging roaring lion, uncontrollable, and ready to bite your head off.

I was the oldest of four and the only girl. I had my own room, which was a safe place for me to run and hide whenever that family member would be in our home. I remember in my room having my imaginary friends I would talk to in the mirror. I would tie a white t-shirt on my head and pretend it was long blond hair and have dinner parties with my bears or dolls. This act would seem harmless, but it was molding me into not loving myself, but desiring to be someone else. I did this for a long time, I don't even remember when I stopped.

I remember when I was in high school, I wasn't having the imaginary friends and t-shirt on my head anymore. I see now how I really wanted to be someone else and live a different life. I would always ask how and why I was put in this family or why things were allowed to happen to innocent children? By this point, I didn't trust people, surely not family, and still the dots were not all connected for a clear picture.

I had my first son when I was twenty years old and my second son when I was twenty-six. Both children have different fathers, but the patten in the relationships was the same. Three years into the relationship, a child was born, and somewhere around the fourth year of the relationship, my child was turning two years old, I left the relationship. Yes, marriage was discussed, but I knew deep down, neither of the men would become my husband. Their inability to be faithful and committed to the relationship were their biggest problems.

I never knew there were many layers of brokenness in my life. Now with two children, I was working being a very independent mom; partying and drinking, played a big role in my life weekly. I did some drugs, sleeping around using men to do things for me, knowing my motives was negative and evil to use them up. I wasn't even aware I was doing that at the time. I even had men doing things for me hoping they wouldn't want to sleep with me.

I had one keeping my vehicle clean, one keeping my boy's haircut, just doing whatever I wanted, with no intentions on doing anything sexual and surely not a relationship. I know now when I look back on it, hurt people really do hurt people. I used to say I haven't hurt anyone, but I did in many ways, and sometimes the other person wasn't even aware.

When I hit my late thirties, things began to shift and change in my life. I moved back to Tennessee. Approximately after two years back in Tennessee, I started a new relationship, and made the decision to get back into church, which is where I was introduced to having a relationship with God that I never knew existed.

The people at this church became family to me, which I greatly needed at that time. They even made me be a hugger and love people more, which was very challenging for me. Creating this intimate relationship with God shifted me to a whole new place in my personal life, family life, and business. God's super was connected to my natural and a new person was found.

I spent the next ten to twelve years at that church crying
tears of joy for so much gratitude towards God's protection
and covering over my life. He transformed so many areas
in my life over those past twelve years, where the enemy
tried to kill me the past thirty. After I started viewing
things from God's perspective, and hearing His voice, I
became obedient to the full revelation God had for my life.
I felt so free. I knew I still had a process to go through, but
just seeing the other side felt so good to know how to fight
the enemy through prayer, praise, and worship. I realized
that I am victorious and that I am being stretched for His
greatness in the earth and for His glory. What a masterpiece
I am becoming!

Michelle Walker, MBA

Co-Founder of Miracles Outreach CDC, Inc.
Founder of WOW Coaching & Consulting

Michelle Walker, MBA is the Co-founder and Executive Director of *Miracles Outreach Community Development, Inc*. Miracles Outreach is a non-profit (501-c3) organization whose primary focus is children who are homeless, abused or victims of Human Trafficking. She is also the *Founder of WOW Coaching and Consulting.*

Michelle holds an MBA from Springfield College. She is also a Minister, certified Life Coach, Victim Advocate, Relationship and Business Consultant. She enjoys traveling with her husband and spending time with family.

Michelle's belief: All things are possible through God. To Whom much is given much is required.

Contact 813-374-2184/mwalker@miraclesoutreach.org
www.Miraclesoutreach.org

I AM GOD'S MASTERPIECE

"Broken Pieces to Masterpiece" has been a challenging topic for me. Various times I have found myself in a state of brokenness, incapable of seeing beyond the shame. Broken so many times in my life, I stopped counting. Sometimes feeling completely shattered and that my situations were beyond repair, or that I didn't even deserve a second chance. Thankfully God has a way of taking those broken pieces and putting them back together again. Broken at the age sixteen and being pregnant, dropping out of college, married at the age of nineteen and divorced at twenty-three, and dealing with infertility at the age of thirty. He has shown me time and time again that He is a God of restoration and there is nothing too hard for Him. This is a just a snapshot of my journey.

Looking back to being sixteen and pregnant, I can recall feeling as if there could not be restoration from my situation. The disappointment I caused my parents and family was a tough pill to swallow. Being the first teenage parent was humiliating. Could you imagine the feeling? Around this time of my life, I was extremely confused. I began doubting myself and my self-worth.

Frequently, I believed I was not capable of love or forgiveness. I thought God could not forgive me, nor could the people I adored the most. There was no justification for my behavior because I knew better. Growing up, I would hear the phrase, "anything done in the dark will come to light." Multiple times going through this process, I considered having an abortion. I reached one of the lowest points in my life; there was no way out of the hole I had dug for myself. I made an appointment at the clinic and went. I cannot describe what transpired that day, but I got up from the chair, walked out of the clinic, and did not return. I sat in the car with my at-the-time boyfriend and told him I could not go through with the plan. Since I did not stay, we knew we had to confide in our families. That was one of the most frightening moments of my life.

Three months passed, and I attended another school for teen mothers. After delivering my daughter towards the end of my junior year, everyone was on summer break. I got acclimated to the swing of things and eventually returned to my primary school. It was challenging being a teen mother. It was all about sacrifice. I had played a sport each year of high school and worked part-time, but instead of doing those things, I put my daughter first. There was a balance that I needed to maintain, and it was demanding. I worked on the weekend, quit softball, and did not attend the functions I usually would have. During this time, I continued to pray and speak life into myself. I knew I could not and would not become another statistic. I would not be an uneducated parent, I would not continue the cycle of having multiple children, and I would not be on welfare.

When my daughter was a few months old, I recall rocking her to sleep in the middle of the night. My father came into the living room. He sat with me and asked me what was on my mind. I began weeping and told him I was sorry for disappointing him, the family, and God. I continued to look in the rear-view mirror and only saw my failures. He embraced me and changed my thought process, all with a few words. He informed me that they had already forgiven me, as God did. Ultimately, the only person keeping me from peace was myself. I heard him, but I did not receive it in my heart. Nevertheless, I began praying on this conversation and realized that if I did not forgive myself, it did not matter what anyone else said or did. Forgiveness has never been a simple task for me. I did not turn the other cheek. Therefore, forgiving myself would be an even harder achievement.

After graduation, my parents encouraged me to follow my dreams of going to college and insisted they would care for my daughter. I decided that I would not go away to college at that time, however the next year I decided to go to Tallahassee for college, and my boyfriend was away at college in Texas. I missed my daughter and knew I could not stay away any longer. It had been eight months, so I came home; I felt like I had abandoned my child and was an awful mother. I did not obtain my degree. When I returned home, I worked a full-time job to provide for my daughter and myself.

My boyfriend and I encouraged and supported each other. Eventually, we agreed that we wanted to be a family, and we got married. I transferred my job, and we found a place in Daytona. Subtly I recognized a change in my husband. The saying "sometimes you wake up and do not recognize the individual you are lying next to," is very accurate. I realized that he was different after his father had passed, so I gave him the benefit of the doubt, but he began to drink constantly and discreetly smoke. One evening, he was drunk and placed his hands on me for the first time.

We had gotten into an altercation, and I began to walk away. Before this night, he had never aggressively grasped me. Whereas that night, he did. He grabbed my arm, and I asked him what he was doing and swung at him. That night he ended up leaving, and I did too. I came back, we worked through our issues, and he apologized. Yet he still continued to drink. We had money to pay the bills, but we did not have the funds for him to drink our money away.

I checked out of our relationship prior to the upcoming incident. But I reached my breaking point two years into the marriage. On a Saturday afternoon, my husband came into the house intoxicated. I was significantly broken at this point in my life and felt as if I had nothing to lose, even though I had the world to lose. We got into a physical altercation until a neighbor knocked on the door. I answered, and she said she heard a lot of commotion. She asked if I was okay, and I told her what happened, and she called the police. My ex-husband left, and I remained there until the cops arrived.

After that day, I knew that I had enough, and I was leaving. We separated eventually, but we did not get a divorce until nearly two years later. I could not believe it. I was not only the first teen parent but also the first individual in my household to have a divorce. If I was not ashamed before, I most definitely was mortified now.

Although I was embarrassed, I knew that I had to put my sanity first. I had to relearn how to pray and focus on hearing God's voice. Often my dad would tell me that God speaks to each person individually; you just have to be open to listening. He could speak through scripture or in a still voice, and along the way, he would send confirmation. Although I had numerous setbacks, I realized they were a part of a bigger picture that I could not see at the time.

I believed that these defeats would keep me from achieving my goals, but in reality, God was using my pain to reveal himself in my life. I had to become self-aware and pinpoint healthy and harmful characteristics to heal. God revealed himself and made it evident that he had never abandoned me. Psalms 119: 105 NIV says, "Your word is a lamp for my feet, a light on my path."

Once I recognized who and whose I was, it was a game changer. I worked on becoming the person God formed me to be. I had to let go of the baggage weighing me down, forgive myself, and release the chains that tied me down mentally and physically. No longer was I held down from the shame of my past, I was free and looking into the future. During this time, my best friend introduced me to the man who is now my best friend, soul mate, and husband of 25 years.

Three years into my new marriage, I was happy and enjoying life, and ready to add to our family. That excitement quickly changed for me and once again, I found myself in a place of brokenness. Dealing with infertility, unable to get pregnant, we tried several different alternative procedures, but they were to no avail. We knew that there were other options such as foster or adoption but were not sure which way we wanted to go, if any. I was mentally and physically drained. The bottom line was, I was unable to have any children and as difficult as it was I had to accept that fact and trust God to heal my heart in this process.

I know that God predestined our relationship, not just in marriage, but also in community and ministry. Once I realized that everything in my life would be used as a testimony and a way to help others in the same position I was once in, my life completely changed. Understanding that throughout my entire life, God was creating this masterpiece.

In every area of my life that I considered broken, God allowed me to go back and serve. As a teen parent, I never imagined myself returning to the same school I attended to become a mentor to young females in the same situation that I was in years prior. I ended up going back to college and completed my bachelor's degree, and two years later earned my master's degree. Also working with single mothers who want to follow their dreams, I have learned to forgive others in a way I never imagined possible, and most importantly myself.

God went as far as blessing my husband and me with children that we could not have ourselves. We established Miracles Outreach Community Development Center in 2001 to help children and families by providing mentoring programs and shelter to youth ages 13-17 for the past 21 years, who have been victims of Trafficking, and any form of abuse. I have learned that through any amount of brokenness, God can create something whole.

Angela Wiafe

Intro and Professional Career Platform:

Founder and CEO, Nephesh In-Bloom

'A Living Soul in Constant Season'

"Never give up, never give in, and never go back. You've got greatness on your inside and greater ahead of you. YOUR best is definitely yet to come. Just keep moving forward, one step at a time."

Angela resides in England with her family. She is a mother of three, an Author and a Poet, a Speaker, Coach, a certified CPD Elite Sales Specialist & Consultant, an Independent Beauty Consultant, and an Entrepreneur.

Nephesh In-Bloom, Ministry Business Info:

Instagram & Facebook - ANGELA Nephesh In-Bloom

WhatsApp - +4479 3014 6486

Email - innephesh247@gmail.com

I AM GOD'S MASTERPIECE

I have been through some dark places in my young adult life. Experiences that left me broken in ways that I never thought or imagined my life to be in, especially having grown up in the church choir all my life. I had no self-love and couldn't even talk about my painful experiences and brokenness with anyone or family. At that time, I felt ashamed, unloved, and unworthy.

Even in this very moment of writing this piece, I had not spoken to my dad who I hold in high regard about it; because I was afraid of being judged and criticized, so I kept this secret. Until the moment that I allowed myself to open up and wholly surrender to God, I never would have experienced true healing and restoration beyond my imagination. Maybe you are in that kind of situation or have experienced it in some way, and you feel broken, unloved, and unworthy. I am here to be your signpost, pointing you in the only way and direction you will ever need on your journey to being restored from broken pieces to God's great masterpiece.

I was raised in a broken home. My parents were never married, so for the most part of my childhood, I was raised by several maternal aunts in Ghana- West Africa. I frequently had to move from one aunt to the next since my mum had travelled to the UK to seek greener pastures when I was about 5 years old. For the better part of my childhood into early teenage life, it was rough and tough, forcing me to quickly grow up in order to face the harsh realities that surrounded me and to fit in.

Whenever I was about to be grounded in life, my foster family had to move me around. My philosophy at that time was to make lemonade when life handed me lemons and limes. I always had to make do with what I got, in order to get the most out of my life. Things kept happening TO me instead of FOR me. I lived a life with no sense of entitlement to anything, but only a strong desire and a hunger to have and own my personal stuff.

Living a life of instability without the proximity of a father's presence, love and guidance greatly affected how I related to men and people in general while growing up. I learned how to survive by being a people pleaser to avoid any kind of confrontations, rejection and hurt. This didn't bode well for me because it meant I couldn't say no even in uncompromising situations, and I had to live in constant fear of rejection.

I was finally reconnected to my dad when I had to leave my junior aunty and travel several States down south to begin senior secondary school. I have been through great depression and rejection by close 'family,' friends and loved ones who were supposed to have been my bedrock and place of comfort. All my life I tried to 'see no evil, do no evil, speak no evil and hear no evil'. However, so great was this pain and hurt that I literally became a living dead, a ghost-shell of my former self, just going through the motions.

Until I arose and said to myself ENOUGH of this! No more! I'll take a stand with the God who answers by fire, the ONLY TRUE LIVING GOD! So, I sought the Lord in prayer and a few RIGHTEOUS men of God stood with me in fervent prayer and fasting. Unbeknownst to me, I was so entangled in a demonic spiritual marriage that was physically manifesting and sabotaging my life, especially my relationships and finances.

All this while I was still growing up in the church, singing in the choir and doing what I thought was good in my own sight, and more than most. I sowed my seed offerings and gave my tithes and was the good individual I needed to be to survive instead of living a fulfilling life. I operated in the 'see no evil, speak no evil and do no evil'. I was an introvert and a people pleaser at that time and would do anything pleasing to others just to avoid confrontations. I was plagued with demonic sexual dreams all the time. All because I received a word of prophecy that I was to wed a man of God, and that I was going to be 'the Joseph' of my family, and the enemy was fighting for that Word not to manifest.

In as much as I tried to stay in the right path (according to my own understanding), I always found myself entangled in bad relationships where all the guys did was take, take, and take. My peripheral environment was almost 80% single parenthood especially on my maternal side - the females had several baby fathers with hardly any stable male presence. I was very determined not to end up like any of those statistics. However, no matter how hard I tried (by my own strength and understanding), the men I encountered were players and married men.

My lack of a father's love, affection and attention meant that I was seeking all those things elsewhere, wherever I could find it, with whomever could give it, whether it was good or not. I couldn't say no to anyone who would show me a little affection. This meant that I couldn't voice out my own opinions. Others spoke for me whether I agreed with their views or not. I couldn't stand rejection and the fact that I didn't FIT IN. It was all about pleasing whoever held my regard. Throughout this complicated mess, I was always on the lookout for a meaningful long-term relationship. I was always desiring more from my relationships, which meant those relationships could never quench the thirst, nor satisfy the hunger I felt deep within. I still felt alone both inside and in the mist of people.

My brokenness fully matured and manifested in two of my prominent relationships. The first was with a guy who got me pregnant, told me he wasn't ready for that kind of responsibility and advised me to abort. He didn't even attend the clinic with me and left me to have the abortion all by myself. I later discovered that, back at the time, on the day of my appointment, he was in France having fun with his ex-girlfriend. This added salt to injury as he broke up with me on the day of my university final year exams, which coincidentally was also the day my maternal grandma had died. I was devastatingly broken and shattered on all sides. I couldn't even tell anyone about my situation, so I internalized my pain, hurt, depression, you name it. Through it all, I was still serving as a choirester at church.

A couple of years down the line I met another guy who I thought was going to marry me. That relationship also didn't last after almost two years together. We had an abortion (second time for me but a first time for him). All because of a misunderstanding. Now according to him he felt that I had hurt him, so he went behind me to inform my mum about my first abortion (but left out the fact that he had done the same with me. I had so many insults and shame-talk from my mum at that time. Immediately after the end of that relationship, I lost my then entrepreneurial businesses, got demoted in my job at that time and generally lost everything that was of 'value' to me besides my faith. I became depressed and withdrawn. I just went through the day-to-day motions. I had lost my glory and I gave up on life. I basically became the living dead as an empty shell of my former self.

I spoke with a pastor friend of mine at that time who revealed to me that I was under the influence of spiritual marriage, and prayed with me over my abortions, sins, and to break the enemy's hold on my life. We went through a period of serious and intense prayers, and deliverance. Then one night I went on YouTube to play some worship music and one of the songs that played from the playlist was by Kari Jobe -I know that you are for me. I know that you will never forsake me in my weakness, and I know that you have come now even if to wipe away my last to remind me of who you are'.

The bible says in Psalm 51:17 and Psalm 34:18 that God does not despise a broken and contrite spirit and is nigh unto to them and saves them. Psalm 66:18 also says if I regard iniquity in my heart, the Lord will not hear me. From that time onwards, I was broken before the Lord and my love for him was rekindled on a much deeper level. My glory started returning gradually every time I was in God's presence.

Then came what I thought was a set-back (at that time), but upon reflection later realized it was God's set-up for a come-back and recompense. I got pregnant again for the third time BUT THIS TIME AROUND, I vowed to myself that I was going to take a chance on the one true living God, on the God who answers by fire like in 1 Kings 18:20-21 when Elijah confronted the children of Israel and the prophets of Baal on Mount Carmel. Elijah said to them that let us call to our various God concerning this sacrifice and the God who answers by fire, let him be God. Now we all know how that story went down in the bible. YHWH (Yah -Jehovah) showed up and proved himself.

I was determined to keep this child at all costs. Ha-ha, My God! I informed the father of the child, and he said to me not to worry because he will do what was right by me, for he also acknowledges that he had sinned against God. Long story short, there were many voices trying to separate us, but he stood his grounds and we're now married with three beautiful kids. We chose names for these kids that reflects God's power, gracious favor, and our thanks to Him, reminding us of the journey and how far God has brought us by His mighty power!

One of my favorite quotes from Dr. Tony Evans says, "Sometimes God lets you hit rock bottom so you will discover that HE IS the Rock at the bottom' and 'the quickest way for God to get you where He wants you, is for Him to be able to use you where He has you." Since I made that stance with God, I've grown both physically and spiritually but especially spiritually, to realize that the value of my life is how much of God I carry daily on the inside, and how much positive and influential impact I make to others, is how much of God (or Jesus) people see in me and how much difference He has made in my life.

I feel like God (in the lyrics of minister Dunsin Oyekan's song) is saying to his people and the world that, "'I want you AT ALL COST, in your fullness and glory. I need you AT ALL COST in your fullness and glory." God is saying with his arms stretched out, that He wants us, his people, (to come to him with all our broken and fractured pieces, our weaknesses and hurts, our pains, and whatever situations we may be going through) to manifest our fullness and glory IN Him, as per His original intention, when he made man in his own image and likeness.

He knows us far better than we could ever know ourselves and he understands your situation much deeper and better that anyone else could, even ourselves. Ephesians 5:14-17 says 'ARISE you who sleep with the dead and Christ will give you life...to walk circumspectly.

There is an urgency in Isaiah 52:1-10 GNTD to wake up from any spiritual sleep/slumber/ignorance and put on strength '....., be strong and great again! Holy city of God, clothe yourself with splendor! The heathen will never enter your gates again. 52:1. We need to ARISE in the knowledge of him, becoming aware and of the fact that we're lost without Him. It is His breath that gives us life as He created. We cannot do anything without him, who is the Creator and Giver of Life.

When we come into that realization, we'll understand that nothing can prevent the Sovereign Lord from delivering us, the apple of his eyes. We're made in His image and likeness, His reflection here in earth, and He will give life for our sake. He will dethrone kings and queens for our sake if He can have us all to himself. For if He did not withhold his only begotten son, but gave him up as the sacrificial lamb for the atonement of our sins, then what else will he withhold for us? If we as parents know how to give our children the best in life, then WHAT can He, the Father of all creation, not do, undo, re-do and overdo? Whatever it takes! WHATEVER IT TAKES, AT ALL COST, if only we will surrender our everything to him. Then, he will take our brokenness as the Creator and Porter that He is, and mold us into HIS masterpieces.

The bible says 'if any man be in Christ, he is a new creation. Old things (previous moral and spiritual condition) have passed away and ALL things have become new (a reawakening of the spirit renews and reforms a new creature altogether, a new life empowered by the HOLY SPIRIT)' (2 Corinthians 5:17). This newness only comes about if and when we are immersed totally, wholly, and deeply IN Christ the Messiah.

There is greater inside of us as God's representatives on earth. There is more - a FULLNESS - in need of manifestation. Yes, we may be broken, battered, abused, misused and unrecognizable pieces, but have we forgotten that HE IS THE POTTER, and we are the clay? Is there any situation (or power) that is too great for Him? Check his track record from old. Take a front row seat and hand over your situation to Him and test Him in this. He is

112

faithful. He is reliable. He is dependable. You can bank on HIS WORD.

Come taste and see that the Lord is good! And I, Angela Abena Adjeiwaa Wiafe, as the redeemed of the Lord, I say so! His word says that He, himself will be a wall of consuming fire round about you, and the glory in the mist of you. He's reaching out to you today, do not harden your heart. Reach out your hand to him and say 'Lord, I want you AT ALL COST, in your fullness (YHWH/YAH/JEHOVAH) and glory. I need you - as the deer pants for water- at all cost, in your fullness and glory.'

Just 'enough' is not enough, won't be enough to manifest as his masterpiece. We want the fullness of his masterpiece, and the presence of God makes that difference. With His presence and IN His presence, anything can happen, and everything is possible. God's presence in our lives is the difference from brokenness to great masterpieces. He is our glory and the lifter of our heads.

About the Author, Dr. Angella Banks

EXPERTISE & TOPICS

I have 20+ years in corporate and community leadership, entrepreneurship, and education. Through my works and partnerships, I've helped several leaders, entrepreneurs, dreamers, ministries, and organizations reach pivotal points of success. I hold a Doctorate in Business Administration (DBA) with a Marketing Specialization. Through my unique mixture of both professional and personal experiences, I am able to quickly identify strategies to meet the specific needs of the audience. I have received rave reviews on my warm down to earth personality, which allows me to easily connect and adapt to almost any culture and environment. Here are some most requested topics:

7 Pillars to PowerLeadership   The Power Leaders Program

Our society today is facing some of its most critical times! When we examine the core of some of these drivers, poor leadership skills will surely surface as a cause. I travel across the country training leaders in (7) key areas: business, education, government, entertainment, spiritual, media, and the arts. Through education and application, individuals are able to see themselves as powerful agents of change.

Dream it! Be it! Live it!

Using my signature brand of "iDream Big," I share my journey of quitting a full-time job at a Fortune 500 company, with no savings, and as a single mother to pursue a dream. I share strategies of how if you Dream it, one day you have to Be it, and then ultimately take ownership to Live it Out!

Request Your Specialized Topic

For booking visit: www.drangellabanks.org

Made in the USA
Middletown, DE
29 December 2022

20676964R00070